The GREAT NIJINSKY

Painting of Vaslav Nijinsky as the Faun

The
GREAT
NIJINSKY

GOD *of* DANCE

LYNN CURLEE

Charlesbridge
TEEN

for NICHOLAS

and in memory of John

The original paintings by Lynn Curlee are acrylic on canvas and are life-size.
The artist would like to thank Dan Arnold for photographing the more recent paintings.

Text and illustrations copyright © 2019 by Lynn Curlee
All rights reserved, including the right of reproduction in whole or in part in any form.
Charlesbridge and colophon are registered trademarks of Charlesbridge Publishing, Inc.

At the time of publication, all URLs printed in this book were accurate and active. Charlesbridge and the author
are not responsible for the content or accessibility of any website.

Published by Charlesbridge
85 Main Street, Watertown, MA 02472
(617) 926–0329 • www.charlesbridgeteen.com

Library of Congress Cataloging-in-Publication Data
Name: Curlee, Lynn, author.
Title: The great Nijinsky : god of dance / Lynn Curlee.
Description: Watertown, Massachusetts : Charlesbridge, [2019] | Audience: Ages: 12+
Identifiers: LCCN 2018019950 (print) | LCCN 2018024428 (ebook) | ISBN 9781632896391 (ebook) |
    ISBN 9781632896407 (ebook pdf) | ISBN 9781580898003 (reinforced for library use)
Subjects: LCSH: Nijinsky, Vaslav, 1890–1950—Juvenile literature. |
    Ballet dancers—Russia (Federation)—Biography—Juvenile literature. |
    Choreographers—Russia (Federation)—Biography—Juvenile literature.
Classification: LCC GV1785.N6 (ebook) | LCC GV1785.N6 C85 2019 (print) | DDC 792.8092 [B] —dc23
LC record available at https://lccn.loc.gov/2018019950

Printed in China
(hc) 10 9 8 7 6 5 4 3 2 1

Illustrations done in acrylic on canvas
Display type set in Yana by Laura Worthington
Text type set in Adobe Garamond Pro
Color separations by Colourscan Print Co Pte Ltd, Singapore
Printed by 1010 Printing International Limited in Huizhou, Guangdong, China
Production supervision by Brian G. Walker
Design and hand lettering by Taline Boghosian

Nijinsky at the peak of his artistry and fame, 1912

Contents

Nijinsky in his final year as a ballet student, 1906

Prologue

Wonder of Wonders

My senses were all blurred that night. The familiar barriers between the stage and the audience were broken. . . . The stage was so crowded with spectators that there was hardly room to move. . . . Hundreds of eyes followed us about. . . . "He is a prodigy" and awed whispers "It is she!" . . . Somebody exquisitely dressed staunched the blood trickling down my arm with a cobwebby handkerchief—I had cut myself against Nijinsky's jeweled tunic. . . . Somebody was asking Nijinsky if it was difficult to stay in the air as he did while jumping; he did not understand at first, and then very obligingly: "No! No! Not difficult. You have to just go up and then pause a little up there."

—Tamara Karsavina

Paris
May 18, 1909

ON A BALMY EVENING IN LATE SPRING, the Théâtre du Châtelet was booked to capacity, with nearly three thousand people in the audience. A troupe of dancers from the legendary Russian Imperial Ballet, the czar's own dance company, was about to appear for the first time in the cultural capital of the Western world, and this preview performance was the hottest ticket in town.

As the theater slowly filled, the sophisticated crowd was keen with anticipation, chatting excitedly among themselves. The famous and the talented, the wealthy and the powerful, the fashionable and the beautiful—all in formal evening dress—filled the orchestra seats and the dress circle above. The crème de la crème of Parisian high society held court from their private boxes. Middle-class patrons of the arts decked in their Sunday best occupied the lower balconies, while artistic young bohemians wearing shabby dark clothing and scarves around their necks found a place in the cheap upper tiers.

The atmosphere was festive. Fresh paint had brightened up the old theater, along with new scarlet velvet hangings and crimson carpeting. The management had the inspired idea to seat only beautiful young women in the first row of the dress circle's sweeping curve, giving out tickets to selected actresses and dancers. As the audience assembled, the dazzling sight of all sixty-three young ladies seated in the "diamond horseshoe" created a sensation. Blondes alternated with brunettes and redheads, all with hourglass figures and low-cut gowns in the style of the belle epoque. Pale bare shoulders were set off by glittering diamonds and lustrous pearls, and elaborate hairstyles featured egret and ostrich plumes.

The year before, a Russian opera company had traveled to Paris and created a sensation with a lavish production of an opera never before seen in the

West—*Boris Godunov*, by Modest Mussorgsky. This tragic story of a medieval Russian czar electrified jaded Parisians with its exotic subject, gorgeous music, splendid singing, and magnificent stagecraft. Russian opera had returned for a second season, and now Russian ballet was about to be added to the mix.

At exactly half past eight, after the traditional three raps from backstage, the lights slowly dimmed, and the restless audience settled down. The conductor tapped his baton on the music stand to cue the orchestra, and with a soft roll of the kettledrum, the music began.

The curtain rose on *The Pavilion of Armida*, a confection of a ballet about a Gobelins tapestry that comes to life. Costumes and decor were in the style of the eighteenth-century French court, and for the second scene, two real fountains with water piped in from the Seine flanked the stage. The audience was swept away by the spectacle.

Eventually a young man took the stage with two ballerinas for a pas de trois. The precision and beauty of the routine riveted the audience. They had never before seen dancing like this. In French ballet, male dancers, when they appeared at all, merely supported the ballerinas, but this dance was centered upon the youth, who moved with such passion and athletic power that a murmur swept the crowd. At the end, instead of gracefully walking off with his partners, the young man impetuously leaped offstage. The audience gasped as they saw him go up into the wings, where they could not see him come down—it was as though he'd taken flight. After a stunned pause, a tremendous wave of applause rolled across the footlights.

Then the dancer returned for his solo—a thrilling series of pirouettes and high jumps, during which he seemed to float suspended in midair. The audience cheered. After solos by the two ballerinas, all three dancers returned for a reprise before taking their bows to a thunderous ovation. When the lights came up at the intermission, the audience scanned their programs to find out about the young man. His name was Vaslav Nijinsky.

———— ✧ ✧ ✧ ————

The next performance that night was the hour-long second act from the opera *Prince Igor*, by Alexander Borodin. The curtain rose to reveal an encampment on the Russian steppes—an immense, desolate landscape of rolling hills beneath a golden sky with pink clouds and plumes of smoke rising from the tents of the Polovtsi, a Tatar tribe. After a lot of impassioned singing, the climax of the act featured the corps de ballet in an epic spectacle of choreography known as the "Polovtsian Dances." Colorfully garbed groups of warriors, slaves, men and women, boys and girls joined in a frenzied climax accompanied by chorus and full orchestra with pounding drums and clashing cymbals. The audience went wild.

Everyone was aware that something extraordinary was happening. In France the ballet had come to be "regarded as a frivolous art form unsuited to serious artistic expression." The Russians were a revelation. During the second intermission, some bolder members of the audience invaded backstage to watch from the wings, wanting to see the dancers up close.

The final act of the evening was *A Banquet*. The curtain rose on a magnificent medieval Russian banquet hall as the setting for a series of dances choreographed to music by different Russian composers. Nijinsky appeared in a segment of *A Banquet* called "The Lezginka," his face painted dramatically and sporting a rakish mustache. He danced the lezginka, a folk dance performed by a group of men in high boots. For the segment titled "The Golden Bird," Nijinsky returned with one of his partners from *The Pavilion of Armida*, Tamara Karsavina. They performed a lovely, intricate pas de deux, he dressed and bejeweled as a Turkish prince, and she as a bird with flaming ostrich feathers. Once again, the audience was dazzled by their virtuosity, and most particularly by Nijinsky's power, grace, and charisma. One spectator said about their impact, "When those two came on, Good Lord! I have never seen such a public. You would have thought their seats were on fire." To conclude the long evening, the entire company paraded to a march by Tchaikovsky, the best known of the Russian composers. This grand finale brought down the house amid a hail of cheers and bravos. The audience demanded seemingly endless curtain calls.

The legend of Vaslav Nijinsky as the greatest of all dancers began with that first spontaneous leap offstage in *The Pavilion of Armida*. It has been said of that glamorous night that "Nijinsky took off his costume, removed his make-up; and went out to supper and fame." When notices of the evening were published in the newspapers, the critics hailed the Russian ballet as spectacular entertainment—a triumph of Russian art—and compared the event to a royal fete at the court of King Louis XIV. The music, the costumes, the decor, and all the featured dancers were singled out for praise. Tamara Karsavina was astonished to discover that she was now "La Karsavina." And Vaslav Nijinsky was immediately hailed as a phenomenon—a "wonder of wonders," and even "God of the dance." He was twenty years old.

SERGEI DIAGHILEV *presents* VASLAV NIJINSKY

in his PARIS DEBUT

"No one thought that in the realm of art there might be something utterly new under the sun when, in instant splendor, there appeared the phenomenon of the Ballets Russes."

ANNA DE NOAILLES, WRITER

THE PAVILION OF ARMIDA

MUSIC BY Nikolai Tcherepnin • CHOREOGRAPHY BY Mikhail Fokine
STORY BY Alexandre Benois • DESIGN AND COSTUMES BY Léon Bakst

INSTEAD OF WALKING off the stage like his partners, Nijinsky, in the role of Armida's Slave, spontaneously leaped into the wings, stunning the crowd.

"THE LEZGINKA"
FROM *A Banquet*

MUSIC BY Mikhail Glinka
CHOREOGRAPHY ADAPTED FROM Marius Petipa BY Mikhail Fokine

THE LEZGINKA was a choreographed version of a rousing Russian folk dance with concise steps and strong movements, traditionally performed by a troupe of men in boots.

"THE GOLDEN BIRD"
FROM *A Banquet*

MUSIC BY Pyotr Ilyich Tchaikovsky • CHOREOGRAPHY BY Marius Petipa

THE GOLDEN BIRD was a classic duet taken from Petipa's masterpiece, *The Sleeping Beauty*, first performed in 1890. Nijinsky, in a bejeweled tunic, and Karsavina, in flaming ostrich feathers, caused a sensation in their pas de deux.

VASLAV NIJINSKY

in "The Lezginka"

Young Vatsa in his ballet school uniform, 1900

Born to Dance

VASLAV FOMICH NIJINSKY was the son of dancers. His parents, Tomasz and Eleonora Nijinsky, were originally from Poland. Professional entertainers who traveled around Russia with their own dance troupe, they performed in theaters, opera houses, music halls, and circuses. Tomasz was known for his athletic ability and high jumps.

Vaslav was born in the Ukrainian city of Kiev, most likely in 1889 (the exact year is disputed by historians). He was the middle child. His brother, Stanislav, called Stassik, was four years older. Their sister, Bronislava, was two years younger. Vaslav called her Bronia, and she called him Vatsa—they were best friends throughout his life. The Nijinsky children traveled with their parents from town to town, living in cheap hotels, growing up backstage among performers and the smell of greasepaint. Their father taught them dance steps when they were little more than toddlers, and soon they danced small parts in the dance troupe themselves. Vatsa first appeared onstage when he was just four years old; he performed a simple little folk dance with some other children. When he was seven, Vatsa had his first solo part—a chimney sweep who rescued a dog, a rabbit, a monkey, and a pig from a fire. The theater was in his blood.

Young Vatsa was a rambunctious, hyperactive child. He spent much of his playtime alone. He loved to climb the walls of narrow hotel corridors, inching his way up with his "feet pressed against one wall, hands against the other." He would disappear for hours at a time, and his frantic mother called the police on several occasions to find him. When he eventually turned up, he was beaten, a typical punishment in those days.

When Vatsa was young, tragedy struck the Nijinsky family. Stassik was about six years old when he was gravely injured in a terrible accident. He leaned out an open window, lost his balance, and fell headfirst onto the cobblestones. He was in a coma for several days. It is likely that he suffered brain damage, because he became slow witted and lacked the coordination to dance. The close-knit Nijinsky family was never quite the same.

Having tired of his responsibilities as husband and father, Tomasz ran away with another woman, abandoning his wife and children. Vatsa's heart was broken. His mother was forced to retire from the stage, and they moved to a shabby apartment in St. Petersburg, the capital city of the Russian Empire. They had little money, and Stassik's problems got worse. He became unruly, aggressive toward his brother and sister, and screamed violently at his mother. Eleonora eventually was forced to confine her older son to a mental asylum. She took Vatsa and Bronia to visit on Sundays. For the rest of his life, Nijinsky would be haunted by the specter of his brother's tragic accident and sad life.

Eleonora had ambitions for her two younger children, and she placed her hopes for a better life on them. In 1898, when he was nine, Vatsa auditioned at the Imperial School of Ballet. He was small, slight, quiet, and shy, but the ballet masters knew his father's reputation, and when they saw him jump, they offered Vatsa a place. Later, Bronia was also accepted. Eleonora's children's lives were changed forever. The prestigious school was funded by the czar, and its students were considered members of his civil service. After many years of rigorous training, the most talented graduated to the Imperial Ballet, the official dance company patronized by the czar, his court, the nobility, and the upper crust of Russian society.

The grand master of the Russian Imperial Ballet was a Frenchman. Marius Petipa had come to St. Petersburg in 1847 to dance for the czar and never left. After a few years, he became chief choreographer, and then grand master, a position he held until he retired in 1903. Petipa is one of the most important figures in the history of dance. He choreographed more than sixty ballets, including *The Sleeping Beauty*, *Swan Lake*, and *The Nutcracker*, masterpieces that are still performed today much as Petipa conceived them. He established strict standards and organized the Imperial Ballet School according to rigid principles.

Nijinsky began his studies during the final years of Petipa's long career. It was a perfect match. As one biographer described it, "The coming together of a highly gifted child who needed artistic refinement and a cultural institution that required raw talent could not have been more timely."

Petipa's school was run like a military academy, but instead of soldiers, it produced the best ballet dancers in the world. For the first two years, students lived at home. Those who were invited to continue became full-time residents. Uniforms were worn proudly as a badge of honor. Girls wore ankle-length dresses with black or white aprons, and boys wore woolen shirts and trousers, black belts with copper buckles, blue caps with visors, high-topped black boots, and overcoats with lyres embroidered on the collars. Vatsa loved to swagger about in his uniform as though it were a theatrical costume.

Boys and girls were kept separate, mixing only when they had ballroom-dance classes or appeared onstage as extras—and even then they were not allowed to speak to one another. They lived in dormitories with rows of narrow beds and had classes on different floors.

The dance studios had raked floors, like a stage, and faced a wall of mirrors. Dance masters gave instructions while playing the violin, as students exercised at the barre. One of the students described dance class in winter when the windows in the boys' studio were left open until class began: "In ten minutes, our blood tingled! We had to work to keep warm—and we worked until the heat from our bodies created an aura of steam around us while our breath made us look as though we held white plumes between our teeth."

Aside from dancing and music, students also took classes in French, history, and mathematics. Vatsa was a poor student, not very interested in anything except dance and music. From the start, he loved the strict routine of dance classes, and his teachers were astounded by his rapid progress.

Everyone recognized his talent, but he was not popular with his classmates. Quiet and shy, he was Polish, not Russian, and spoke with an accent. To the other boys, "he seemed almost stupid . . . a slow thinker." He had unusual features, with high, sharp cheekbones and almond-shaped eyes. Sometimes Vatsa got into fights when others bullied him by ridiculing his speech and looks. They taunted him with racial slurs, calling him "Japonczek," or "the little Japese." Jealous of his dance skills, the other boys jeered, "Are you a girl, to dance so well?"

One day the bullying escalated. The boys were practicing jumping outside of class, and while Vatsa wasn't looking, one boy greased the floor with soap. Vatsa slipped, fell, and was seriously injured. He had a lacerated liver and internal bleeding and fell into a coma. At first the doctors weren't sure that he would live. Thankfully, he came around after a few days, but he spent several months in the hospital. One day he witnessed a young man's death in the next bed. Vatsa was affected deeply by his hospital experience, writing later: "I know what death is. Death is a terrible thing. I have felt death many a time. I was dying in a clinic when I was fifteen years old. [In fact, he was only twelve.] I was a brave kid. I jumped and fell. . . . In the hospital I saw death with my own eyes."

Besides working hard to catch up and rebuild his lost muscle tone, Vatsa tried to win over the other boys. "I was ring-leader in many pranks," he wrote later, and once he was suspended for shooting wads of paper at people with a slingshot. But as the school years passed, Vatsa became increasingly dedicated, focusing on his dancing.

Dancers are athletes who train to make extremely difficult movements appear natural and easy. As Vatsa grew, his body was sculpted by rigorous repeated exercises. He was quite short—only about five feet four inches. He had a small head set upon a powerful and expressive neck with sloping shoulders. His upper body was stocky, his arms sinewy, and his hands large. His legs were massive, even for a dancer, his thighs and calves bulging with thick, well-defined muscles. With his Slavic features and dancer's body, Vatsa was growing into an attractive young man.

During his final school years, Vatsa danced for the public as a soloist in many productions. In 1906 he appeared with some of the leading dancers of the Imperial Ballet, an unheard-of honor for a student. After graduation in 1907, he joined the czar's company, but instead of starting in the corps de ballet and moving up the ranks, he immediately was given bigger, more important parts.

That summer Vatsa was contacted by his father, Tomasz, who invited his son to visit. They demonstrated dance steps for each other, and Tomasz gave Vatsa a pair of cuff links. But Vatsa still resented his father's desertion, so it was an awkward reunion. When Tomasz asked his son to meet his new wife, Vatsa stormed out. He never saw his father again.

For the next two years, Vatsa refined his art in a series of roles in major productions, serving as partner for some of the most famous Russian prima ballerinas. By his late teens, Vaslav Nijinsky was the most promising young male dancer in the Russian Imperial Ballet. He had received the best education possible and began his career at the end of the Petipa era, when new ideas were circulating. He was in the right place at precisely the right time.

Autographed portrait of Sergei Diaghilev, 1916

The World of Art

WHILE VATSA WAS A BOY learning his craft at the Imperial Ballet School, a young Russian man was busy making his mark in the world. Sergei Pavlovich Diaghilev was born in 1872, the son of an officer in the Imperial Guard. His mother died soon after he was born from complications suffered during childbirth (it was rumored that the baby's enormous head was the problem, although a common infection was more likely), but his father soon remarried, and young Sergei grew up in a comfortable, loving, and cultured household surrounded by people who appreciated art and music. He initially planned to become a musician, but when he realized his talent was limited, he became more interested in the visual arts. In the 1890s, when he was in his twenties, Sergei fell in with a group of young intellectual writers, musicians, and painters. Diaghilev became their unofficial leader, and in 1898, he and his friends founded a magazine called *World of Art*, which focused on art, architecture, music, literature, philosophy, and theater.

Diaghilev was intelligent, cultured, suave, haughty, and somewhat snobbish. Tall and a bit portly, he indeed had a large head, topped by thick black hair with a startling streak of pure white in front. He was quite the imposing figure. Charismatic, charming, bold, and passionate, he also could be manipulative and ruthless. Diaghilev had a knack for making social connections, recognizing talent, and organizing people. A connoisseur of art and music, he had exquisite taste, coupled with what has been described as "the energy and strategic imagination of a great Russian general, which he placed in the service not of war, or financial conquest, but in the cause of beauty." He also possessed a boundless, optimistic, driving ambition. At the age of twenty-three, Diaghilev described himself in a letter to his stepmother: "First of all I am a great charlatan, although one with flair; second I'm a great charmer; third I've great nerve; fourth I'm a man with a great deal of logic and few principles; and fifth I think I lack talent; but . . . I've found my real calling—patronage of the arts."

His big breakthrough came when he took an exhibition of Russian painting and sculpture to Paris in 1906. The following year Diaghilev returned to Paris to present concerts of Russian music never before heard in the West. Then in 1908, he organized the brilliant season of Russian opera in the City of Light, featuring the production of *Boris Godunov* that created such a sensation among the Parisian cultural elite. By the age of thirty-five, Diaghilev was an international impresario of the arts.

Sergei Diaghilev was also quite openly, even grandly, homosexual. He was well known throughout the underground gay subcultures of St. Petersburg and Paris and dared to make no secret of his sexuality in a time when absolute discretion was required by polite society.

—— ✦✦✦ ——

During his late teens, Vaslav Nijinsky's star was rising at the Imperial Ballet, but otherwise he was naïve and unsophisticated. The narrow curriculum of the Imperial Ballet School had ill prepared him to make his way in the world. He missed the strictly organized routine: "I finished school at the age of eighteen. I graduated and was let out. I did not know what to do because I did not know how to dress. I was used to uniforms. I did not like civilian dress and therefore did not know how to wear it. . . . I felt free but the freedom terrified me. . . . I did not know life."

Vatsa's day-to-day life still centered on ballet class, the daily regimen of exercises at the barre that kept a dancer supple and finely tuned. He also rehearsed and performed in ballets for the czar and his court, and his days were filled with hard but stimulating and rewarding work. To better his financial circumstances, he moved back into a room in his mother's apartment and gave private ballroom-dance lessons to rich, young society girls.

In school Vatsa had crushes on some of his female classmates from time to time—even though they were not allowed to speak—but now Vatsa developed serious feelings for Maria Gorshkova, a beautiful fellow dancer in the Imperial Ballet Company. His mother, Eleonora, strongly disapproved, telling her son that for the sake of his art he must not become involved in love affairs with other dancers. (Perhaps she was thinking of her long-absent husband.) Vatsa ended the romance when it became clear that Maria was interested in him only because of his status in the company. He told his mother, "I had my arms around her and was about to kiss her when she coyly whispered, 'Vatsa, promise me that you will insist on dancing a pas de deux with me'. . . . Now I am cured of love."

Around this time Vatsa had his first sexual experience with a woman. One of his more worldly ex-classmates took him to visit a prostitute. The encounter did not end happily—she gave him gonorrhea. In an era without antibiotics, the accepted treatment for this sexually transmitted disease in Russia involved applying leeches to the testicles, a fairly horrifying and humiliating ordeal. Apparently this drastic cure eventually worked, but only after five long months of regular treatments. In addition to this unpleasant episode, Vatsa also struggled with unusually obsessive guilt over masturbation, a common enough activity, but which at the time was regarded as "self-abuse" and considered to be debilitating physically, causing baldness, rotting teeth, and loss of vigor and stamina. He became convinced that he danced better when he practiced self-control, and on several occasions vowed to give up his solitary habit completely. But abstinence was difficult for him, and whenever he gave in to his urges he suffered terrible remorse.

In the midst of this teenage maelstrom of idealistic devotion to dance, hard work, raging hormones, conflicting emotions, sexual desire, and guilt, young Vatsa met someone who would change his life. In 1907 Prince Pavel Dimitrievich Lvov was thirty years old, the handsome and very well-connected scion of a wealthy noble Russian family. The prince was a patron of the ballet and an avid sportsman. He was one of the first Russians to own an automobile and fly in an airplane. He also was something of a playboy, drawn to athletic young men. After admiring Nijinsky on the stage from afar, he allegedly paid a dancer acquaintance a thousand rubles to arrange an introduction.

Vatsa met the prince for dinner at a fashionable, expensive restaurant. The next day he was summoned to the glamorous establishment of Fabergé, fabled jeweler to the czar and his court, where he was presented with a gold-and-diamond ring from the prince. Such lavish attention was heady, and soon Prince Lvov and Nijinsky became lovers. This kind of sexual relationship was quite common in the theatrical world. Many ballerinas and actresses became mistresses of wealthy upper-class male patrons, and homosexual male patrons were interested in well-built, young male dancers. Prince Lvov showered Vatsa with gifts and introduced him to the pleasures of fashionable clothing, fine dining, and luxurious surroundings. He even helped out with the Nijinsky family finances. The Nijinskys were able to move to a larger apartment, where Prince Lvov outfitted an elegant bedroom and sitting room for Vatsa. Nijinsky could afford to stop teaching dance to society girls, which must have been a relief, since it had always been difficult for him to convey what he wanted from his students.

Surprisingly, Eleonora was thrilled with this new relationship. After years on the road as a dancer, she was wise to the ways of the world and felt that Vatsa's association with an important patron such as Prince Lvov could only advance his career. She became friends with the prince herself, and when he visited he often brought gifts for her and Bronia. Prince Lvov and Vatsa were genuinely fond of each other. Later in life Nijinsky recalled, "He loved me as a man does a boy. . . . He wrote me love poetry. . . . I loved him because I felt that he loved me. I wanted to live with him always because I loved him." Eventually, however, the bloom came off the rose of the romance, and Lvov became restless. Perhaps the reality of Vatsa the person did not match the object of his desire: Nijinsky the dancer. But there had been a real connection between the dancer and the prince, and so Prince Lvov wanted to find a new situation for his young protégé.

Prince Lvov was friendly with Sergei Diaghilev; they traveled in the same upper-crust gay social circles of St. Petersburg and attended the same cultural events. Diaghilev had already met Nijinsky and seen him dance, but now Prince Lvov practically pushed his young friend into Diaghilev's arms. He arranged for Diaghilev to telephone Vatsa and invite him to his hotel. Nijinsky later wrote, "I hated him for his voice, which was too self-assured, but I went in search of luck." By now Vatsa knew very well what was expected of him. "I found luck there because I immediately made love to him. I trembled like an aspen leaf. I hated him, but I put up a pretense, for I knew that my mother and I would starve to death. I understood Diaghilev from the first moment and pretended therefore that I agreed with all his views. I realized that one has to live, and therefore it did not matter to me what sacrifice I made."

As an up-and-comer in the Imperial Ballet, Nijinsky was not likely to starve, and despite his lament of martyrdom, Vatsa made his own decision to connect with Diaghilev. He certainly understood that a liaison might help his career, and soon it became clear that the young artist and mature impresario each had important qualities that fulfilled something in the other. Sergei Diaghilev took the place of Prince Lvov as Vatsa's friend, patron, mentor, and lover, and they began a long-term relationship. The prince withdrew from the situation, and Nijinsky's token of gold and diamond was replaced with an even larger ring of platinum and sapphire from Diaghilev.

Diaghilev and Nijinsky made an odd pair. The imposing Diaghilev, in his heavy, black, fur-trimmed topcoat, complete with bowler, spats, walking stick, and monocle, towered above his smaller, much younger, quieter, and socially awkward companion, who often appeared ill at ease out of his dance attire.

Self-confident and larger-than-life, the worldly older man took complete charge of the couple's life together. Thumbing their noses at convention, the two men eventually lived together openly as a couple, something quite brazen and shocking in the early twentieth century. The whiff of this scandal would follow Nijinsky for the rest of his life and is a cornerstone of his legend.

The relationship may have begun as a mutually beneficial sexual arrangement, but as time went on, the emotional relationship grew. Diaghilev loved and admired Nijinsky's immense talent as well as his dramatically sculpted body and arresting Slavic features, and he came to love the young man himself. He strove to expand the dancer's horizons, exposing him to the wider world of visual arts, music, and literature, and he provided Vatsa with a life of comfort and security.

Upon Nijinsky's triumphant Parisian debut on May 18, 1909, the young dancer went from relative obscurity to being the toast of the City of Light—literally overnight. Just two years out of his sheltered life in school, Vatsa was catapulted into the spotlight of international fame.

Later that summer, following the exhilarating but exhausting season of performances in Paris, Diaghilev took Vatsa, now reveling in the first blush of celebrity, to the Grand Hôtel des Bains in Venice for a kind of honeymoon, along with other members of his entourage. Nijinsky must have caused a sensation when he appeared on Venice's famed Lido beach in a short scarlet bathing costume, without the usual tank top worn by men, his dancer's muscles rippling. In 1909, when properly modest women still wore long skirts to the floor, gentlemen simply did not appear bare-chested or show their naked thighs in mixed company. But Vaslav Nijinsky was no ordinary gentleman. And with a single stroke, Sergei Diaghilev had made him a star.

Painting of Mikhail Fokine as Harlequin in Carnaval

The Ballets Russes

W HEN DIAGHILEV DECIDED to take the Russian ballet to Paris in 1909, he called on old friends from *World of Art* for help. His inner circle included two very accomplished men. Alexandre Benois was an intellectual, artist, art critic, and historian who conceptualized and designed new ballets. He worked closely with Léon Bakst, a talented painter who designed costumes and sets. Diaghilev engaged an ambitious young ballet master from the Imperial Ballet as choreographer. Mikhail Fokine was impatient with the Imperial Ballet's old formulas and traditions, and he was eager for an opportunity to show off his innovative ideas. Under Diaghilev's leadership, the collaboration of Benois, Bakst, and Fokine would transform the art of ballet and bring it into the twentieth century.

Diaghilev and his creative team strove for historical realism in costumes and scenic design. They visited art museums and consulted books for inspiration. Instead of using standard all-purpose tutus and stock backdrops, costumes and sets were well researched and beautifully executed. As choreographer, Fokine abandoned Petipa's reliance on star ballerinas. He constructed his dances to reflect and propel the romance and drama of the story. He used very little toe dancing. His dancers had to be real actors, and the male roles were just as important as the female ones. The combination of great music with virtuoso dancing and acting was magnified by the originality of the fabulous costumes and bold and imaginative scenic designs. Audiences were astonished by the visual spectacle as well as the artistry of the dancing.

Diaghilev wanted only the best dancers, so he recruited his troupe from the Imperial Ballet. Although officially employees of the czar, they were allowed to travel and work abroad during their summers off. Nijinsky was the best of several outstanding male dancers signed by Diaghilev, and the list of talented ballerinas was headed by Tamara Platonovna Karsavina. She was four years older than Nijinsky, and like him, was born to dance. Her father was a principal dancer and later a ballet master with the Imperial Ballet. Unlike Nijinsky, she came from a cultured, intellectual family and had received a well-rounded education. Karsavina was intelligent, modest, refined, and beautiful, but in 1909 she had not yet achieved the status of prima ballerina in the czar's company.

After the stunning impact of his first season of ballet, Diaghilev decided that his pickup dance company would reassemble and return to Paris in 1910 with an even more sensational program. And now he gave the company an official name—the Ballets Russes.

For the second season, Diaghilev and his creative team decided to mount two new major productions along with shorter and smaller works. One of these new ballets was based upon a Russian folktale. *The Firebird* is the charming story of a magic bird that saves the crown prince Ivan from a monstrous ogre and unites him with his princess. Diaghilev wanted to give the sophisticated Parisians another taste of the Russian soul. He commissioned the music from an obscure young Russian composer, Igor Fyodorovich Stravinsky.

Painting of Tamara Karsavina in The Golden Cockerel

Stravinsky was born in 1882. His father was a bass in the Imperial Opera Company, so he grew up surrounded by music. His parents wanted him to study law, but young Stravinsky was irresistibly drawn to music, and once his parents relented, Stravinsky studied theory and composition with the best: Nikolai Rimsky-Korsakov, the leader of the classical music world in Russia. In 1909 Diaghilev was impressed by a performance of one of Stravinsky's student compositions, a piece called *Fireworks*. In a leap of faith, Diaghilev hired the young composer to write the music for *The Firebird*.

Small and wiry but very dapper, Stravinsky was intense and intellectual. He wore round eyeglasses with thick lenses that gave him a perpetually startled, owlish appearance. Igor Stravinsky was twenty-seven years old when he received the commission that would change his life.

Conferring closely with Benois, Bakst, and Fokine, Stravinsky produced a highly original and astonishingly beautiful score that manages to sound traditional and modern at the same time. At the premiere in Paris on June 25, 1910, Tamara Karsavina was the Firebird and Fokine himself danced the part of Prince Ivan. Nijinsky begged Diaghilev to give him the role of the Firebird and wanted to dance the role *en pointe*, which no male dancer had ever done. But this inspired casting idea was abandoned when Diaghilev decided that even the sophisticated Parisian public was not ready to accept the idea of two men performing an inherently erotic pas de deux. As it was, Karsavina performed brilliantly, the ballet was regarded as an instant classic, and Stravinsky suddenly found himself a famous man.

The second new production that year was equally exotic and sensational. *Scheherazade* was a lurid Arabian Nights fantasy set in a sultan's harem, climaxing with an orgy and slaughter, set to the surging music of Nikolai Rimsky-Korsakov. The story was described by one critic: "A harem of beautiful women [use] the absence of their lord and master to indulge in an orgy . . . with a band of muscular Negroes, ending in a blood bath of vengeance."

An orgy was racy stuff to show onstage in 1910, and with Nijinsky in one of his most famous roles as the sultana's Golden Slave, *Scheherazade* was an extravaganza that pushed the outer limits of propriety. The sophisticated Parisians were dazzled and titillated by the risqué spectacle of simulated lovemaking onstage.

Fokine described the effect Nijinsky made as the Golden Slave: "Now he was a half-human, half-feline animal, softly leaping great distances, now a stallion, with distended nostrils, full of energy, overflowing with an abundance of power, his feet impatiently pawing the ground." Another critic wrote: "He was undulating and brilliant as a reptile." Marcel Proust, the great writer, attended the first performance of *Scheherazade*. His comment was simply, "I never saw anything so beautiful."

The Eastern style of Bakst's scenic design and costumes became the rage among Parisian fashionistas. Couturiers made oriental-style gowns, and grande dames wore turbans. Decorators used Bakst's ideas in some of the most fashionable salons, and in homage to the *Scheherazade* color scheme, La Maison Cartier, jeweler of kings, combined sapphires and emeralds in one piece of jewelry for the first time.

The second season in the City of Light was even more successful than the first. The Ballets Russes had triumphed again, and Vaslav Nijinsky was once more its brightest star. As the Golden Slave he radiated a powerful sexual magnetism, and his audiences devoured it. At the same time, the scandalous nature of his private life with Diaghilev was no secret. As Nijinsky became more and more celebrated, shocking rumors circulated "that he was very debauched, that he had girdles of diamonds and emeralds given to him by an Indian prince." Shy, quiet Vatsa was becoming a sexual icon.

JUNE 25, 1910

THE BALLETS RUSSES

presents

THE FIREBIRD

MUSIC BY Igor Stravinsky

CHOREOGRAPHY BY Mikhail Fokine

STORY BY Alexandre Benois

DESIGN AND COSTUMES BY Léon Bakst

*"A very rich and very complete lyrical drama, a rare event for a ballet;
it is alive, expressive, and everywhere full of the most fresh poetry."*

ROBERT BRUSSEL, CRITIC

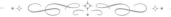

IN AN ENCHANTED FOREST, Prince Ivan captures and releases a Firebird, earning a magic feather. When he comes across thirteen princesses imprisoned by an evil ogre, Prince Ivan uses the feather to summon the Firebird, who casts a spell on the ogre and releases the princesses.

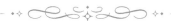

The Parisian audience's first view of the ballet was of a mysterious enchanted forest. When the Firebird appeared and performed a pas de deux with Prince Ivan, the music seemed to shimmer and sparkle, and tender love music played when the prince encountered the princesses.

Then the music turned violent when the evil ogre entered, with jagged, crashing syncopations, before softening into a lullaby as the Firebird lulled the ogre and his minions to sleep. The ballet closed with a grand wedding and coronation pageant, accompanied by a series of thrilling fanfares.

TAMARA KARSAVINA

as the Firebird

THE BALLETS RUSSES

presents

SCHEHERAZADE

MUSIC BY Nicolai Rimsky-Korsakov

CHOREOGRAPHY BY Mikhail Fokine

STORY BY Alexandre Benois

DESIGN AND COSTUMES BY Léon Bakst

"The transport of [Nijinsky's] movements, the encircling giddiness, the dominance of his passion reached such heights that when the executioner's sword pierced him in the final tumult we no longer really knew whether he had succumbed to the avenging steel or to the unbearable violence of his joy."

FRANCIS DE MIOMANDRE, WRITER

THE SULTAN SUSPECTS HIS WIFE, the sultana, of adultery. As a trick, he pretends to go out hunting, but when he returns early to find his harem in the midst of an orgy with their slaves, he slaughters them all on the spot.

*S*cheherazade was an elaborate stage spectacle. The curtain rose on a lavish, vibrant stage—vivid blues and greens clashed with reds, purples, oranges, and yellows. The awe-inspiring effect was achieved by swags of draperies, big pillows, careful lighting, and colorful costumes.

Nijinsky's performance as the Golden Slave was sensational. He performed a sinuous dance of seduction, undulating around the sultana without touching her. Nijinsky's choreographed death included an upside-down pirouette. He spun balanced on the top of his head, his legs extended.

At the premiere the audience was stunned into silence before breaking out into ecstatic applause. The death choreography was an unexpected feat—much like a break-dance move. The ballet sealed Nijinsky's status as a sex symbol.

VASLAV NIJINSKY

as the Golden Slave

Nijinsky in Giselle, *1910*

4

Celebrity and Adulation

AFTER THE INITIAL THRILL, it seems that Nijinsky had no real taste for fame. He was confident of his artistry, and he was well aware of the effect he made onstage, but otherwise he was without much vanity or pretense. A Russian newspaper reporter observed: "Dressed modestly, shy, with a very boyish appearance, Nijinsky did not look like the hero of the brilliant Russian season in Paris. . . . He speaks just like a child. He gets worked up and blushes just as if he is embarrassed by his celebrity." On the other hand, he was totally dedicated to his art—it was his calling and reason for being. To keep this focus, he depended upon Diaghilev to grease the wheels of everyday existence. Nijinsky had few possessions and cared little about money as long as his mother and sister were living comfortably. As Diaghilev's companion, he had no contract and took no salary. Diaghilev had complete control of their life together. It is not surprising that after a few years of white-hot fame, without any real responsibilities beyond those to his art and his career, Nijinsky became somewhat spoiled, difficult, and obstinate. The great Nijinsky was capable of throwing a tantrum, but his demands were usually made in the service of his art.

The Ballets Russes had become the latest rage in Paris, and as its star attraction, Nijinsky was in great demand socially. Everyone wanted to see him up close and in person, and with Diaghilev's considerable gift for maneuvering in society, the couple attended the most important and fashionable events together. They were invited to elaborate dinner parties by grand society matrons and were guests of honor at soirees given by members of the French artistic establishment. A few important patrons were honored with private performances in the intimacy of their own elegant townhouses.

The Russians also were taken up by an elite clique of artistic and intellectual Parisian homosexuals: Marcel Proust, the great novelist who was just beginning to assemble his masterpiece, *In Search of Lost Time*; Reynaldo Hahn, a successful composer, conductor, and music critic, who had been a child prodigy; and Jean Cocteau, poet, artist, future filmmaker, and eventual French cultural icon.

When they first met, Cocteau expressed a desire to work with Diaghilev. The impresario's famous response was "Astonish me!" Cocteau was welcomed into Diaghilev's inner circle, sketched witty backstage caricatures, produced several posters for the Ballets Russes, and eventually developed ideas for new ballets. The same age as Nijinsky, a fascinated Cocteau at first fawned over him, but he became disappointed and a bit exasperated when the dancer responded only with polite indifference.

Many visual artists were inspired by Nijinsky and asked him to pose. One of the most beautiful and evocative images of him is a wonderfully dashing charcoal sketch by John Singer Sargent, the American society portraitist. Nijinsky posed in his costume and makeup from *The Pavilion of Armida*. He wears a jeweled choker high up on his long, expressive neck; his head is raised, his nostrils flared. He looks radiant.

Sketch of Nijinsky in The Pavilion of Armida
by John Singer Sargent, 1911

Another modeling gig didn't go as well. French sculptor Auguste Rodin asked Nijinsky to pose nude for a proposed statue. After a few sessions Diaghilev became suspicious about Rodin's intentions and in a fit of jealousy put an end to the project. Rodin produced only a few small, knobby figurines from his sessions with Nijinsky, rough maquettes for a life-size statue that was never made.

In contrast to the public adulation, many who admired Nijinsky onstage were quite disappointed when they met him. Once, in a fit of pique, Cocteau observed snidely, "One would never have believed that this little monkey with sparse hair, wearing a skirted overcoat and a hat balanced on the top of his head, was the idol of the public." People were always very surprised to discover that the great dancer, so powerful and charismatic onstage, was shy and awkward in social situations. Polish and Russian were Nijinsky's native languages, but his French was only basic, and this isolated him in the Parisian social scene. Aware of his provincial roots, he didn't want to make any faux pas, so he didn't say much. When he did speak, however, he could be very perceptive, and blunt. Once, at a party, he observed that their hostess, a tall and haughty woman, resembled a giraffe. Diaghilev was aghast and apologetic. "No, no," Nijinsky doubled down, "giraffe is beautiful, long, gracious—she looks like it."

Nijinsky was by nature a very private man. He tended to avoid eye contact and often seemed detached or even a bit nervous, with a bad habit of picking at his fingers, which always looked red and raw. It was hard to reconcile this shy, quiet, short, stocky, apparently ordinary, and even somewhat dull young man with the brilliant and glamorous God of Dance who had conquered all of Paris with his charisma and artistry. One of his dancer colleagues said, "Nijinsky, even though he was always surrounded by people, seemed always to be alone; he was incapable of mixing in any way. If he spoke at all . . . he would talk softly and shyly, without looking at the person, and move away as quickly as possible." Some thought him to be a kind of idiot savant, a great genius at one thing only, and otherwise somewhat backward. Benois, Diaghilev's great friend and colleague, found Nijinsky "a rather stocky man, not at all beautifully proportioned, and furthermore so timid that he seemed rather to fade into the background." Many of Diaghilev's friends found him "dull and unintelligent."

But these statements do him a disservice. As an adult Nijinsky became well-read, with a fondness for Tolstoy and Dostoyevsky, and he played the piano quite well. Like many creative people, Nijinsky was an introvert who lived in his own imagination, except when he was performing. Then his almost magical transformation into character was uncanny, and his skill was dazzling.

This transformation rarely happened in rehearsal, where Benois once observed that Nijinsky "performed everything with unfailing precision, but there was something mechanical and automatic in his execution." The real magic required an audience. To prepare himself, Nijinsky had a backstage pre-performance ritual. After arriving at the theater, he changed into rehearsal clothes and warmed up alone. Then he washed and spent a half hour putting on his makeup. He was oblivious to all the inevitable backstage chaos with people milling about. Benois commented that "order ruled in the dressing room, where costumes were hung just so, and sticks of makeup were lined up on the dressing table with military precision." The final metamorphosis took place when Diaghilev's manservant, Vassili, helped Nijinsky into his costume, about which he was always very particular. "At these moments the usually apathetic Vaslav became nervous and capricious. . . . He gradually began to change into another being, the one he saw in the mirror. He became reincarnated and actually *entered into* his new existence."

— ✧✧✧ —

Early in 1911 the Imperial Ballet Theater management suddenly dismissed Nijinsky. The details are unclear, but according to some accounts, he wore "an indecent and improper" costume in a performance attended by the dowager empress, mother of the czar, and she was offended. Some think that this episode was manufactured by the Imperial Ballet as an attempt to bring the famous international star down a notch. Or perhaps the entire incident was orchestrated by Diaghilev so that Nijinsky could dance only for him. Whatever the reason, Nijinsky was fired. But there was an unforeseen consequence—no longer under imperial patronage, Nijinsky was now liable for military service. For the young, sensitive artist, this was unthinkable, and so he left Russia. As a draft dodger, Vaslav Nijinsky was suddenly a young man without a country, and he would live the rest of his life in a kind of self-imposed exile.

Later in 1911 the Russians had their third season in Paris, and they also began appearing in other European capitals, such as Berlin and Brussels. Nijinsky triumphed in three of his very greatest, most iconic roles. He dazzled as Harlequin in *Carnaval*, a ballet featuring well-known characters from the commedia dell'arte, performing their antics to a series of short pieces by German romantic composer Robert Schumann.

Nijinsky created another sensation in *The Specter of the Rose*, a short ballet set to a piece of music called *Invitation to the Dance*, by another German romantic composer, Carl Maria von Weber. The entire ballet is an extended solo with pas de deux that Fokine choreographed specifically for Nijinsky and Karsavina.

Although short, the ballet was very strenuous. Nijinsky was onstage performing extremely difficult choreographic and athletic feats for about ten minutes. Cocteau gives us a vivid recollection of the scene backstage after this ballet, describing stagehands who "squirt water into his face and scrub at him with towels, like a boxer between rounds. What grace coupled with what brutality! I still hear the thunder of that applause, still see that young man smeared with greasepaint, sweating, panting, one hand pressed against his heart and the other clutching a stage brace. He collapsed on a chair, and in a few seconds, slapped, drenched, pummeled, he walked back onstage, bowing, smiling."

For his role as the fragrant specter of the rose, Nijinsky wore a painted body stocking with rose petals of tulle that were sewn onto the costume just before he went onstage. These gossamer petals, stiff with Nijinsky's dried sweat, were gathered up by his dresser, Vassili, after every performance. They made exquisite souvenirs and were collected by ballet groupies of the era. People sometimes even sneaked into his dressing room during performances to steal his underwear! Nijinsky, the sexual icon, had become rock-star famous, worshipped and adored almost unconditionally by his public.

THE BALLETS RUSSES

presents

CARNAVAL

MUSIC BY Robert Schumann
CHOREOGRAPHY BY Mikhail Fokine
DESIGN AND COSTUMES BY Léon Bakst

"An acrobatic cat stuffed full of candid lechery and crafty indifference, a schoolboy, wheedling, thieving, swift-footed, utterly freed of the chains of gravity, a creature of perfect mathematical grace. Desire, mischief, self-satisfaction, arrogance. . . . Such was Vaslav Nijinsky in Le Carnaval, performing while surrounded by an uninterrupted roar of applause."

JEAN COCTEAU, POET, ARTIST, FILMMAKER

INNOCENT, COQUETTISH, GALLANT, AND ROGUISH characters from the traditional commedia dell'arte tease, flirt, couple, fight, and uncouple in a series of light and humorous episodes laced with satire and poignancy.

First produced for a charity benefit in St. Petersburg, *Carnaval* was created and choreographed in only three rehearsals. It premiered in Paris in 1910 with Fokine as Harlequin, but Nijinsky made the role his own when he took over as Harlequin in 1911.

The simple, elegant set consisted of a blue curtain backdrop, two chandeliers, and two small striped sofas. Nijinsky's tights were painted with diamond shapes, and his face was a mask of black greasepaint. He stunned audiences with his virtuoso dancing and acting, ending his solo with a grand pirouette—first spinning rapidly and then more slowly as he lowered himself until he was sitting on the stage floor with legs crossed, facing the audience with an insolent smirk on his face.

VASLAV NIJINSKY

as Harlequin

✦ ✦ ✦

THE BALLETS RUSSES

presents

THE SPECTER OF THE ROSE

MUSIC BY Carl Maria von Weber

CHOREOGRAPHY BY Mikhail Fokine

DESIGN AND COSTUMES BY Léon Bakst

✦ ✦ ✦

*"So loud was the applause after Nijinsky's leap from the window
that the orchestra was unable to finish playing the music."*

SERGE GRIGORIEV, BALLETS RUSSES STAGE MANAGER

A YOUNG WOMAN RETURNS HOME from a ball with a rose and
falls asleep. The rose's spirit appears in her dreams and dances with her
before leaping out the window.

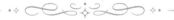

Karsavina, in the role of the Young Woman, was sleeping in her chair when Nijinsky appeared in the window as an androgynous apparition—the Specter of the Rose. He performed an extended solo, then took Karsavina's hand and led her in a waltz. He returned her, still sleeping, to her chair, before executing a spectacular leap out the window. Backstage the scene was not so romantic: an exhausted Nijinsky landed from the leap against a mattress supported by six stagehands.

Nijinsky came to regard *The Specter of the Rose* as overly sentimental, but this tiny ballet created one of his most popular signature roles. Audiences loved the romanticism—at least one grande dame fainted at the premiere, and during other performances, several ladies overcome with emotion had to be led out of the audience.

VASLAV NIJINSKY

as the Specter of the Rose

Painting of Bronislava Nijinska as a street dancer in Petrushka

Petrushka

CARNAVAL and **THE SPECTER OF THE ROSE** were popular crowd pleasers, but Nijinsky's third ballet of 1911 would become a true masterwork. After the success of *The Firebird*, Diaghilev was eager to have more ballets from Igor Stravinsky, and Benois had come up with the idea of a ballet about dancing puppets at a traditional Russian street fair. Stravinsky was working on a piano concerto, but he immediately embraced the commission and collaborated closely with Benois and Fokine to refine the story before beginning to compose. He incorporated the unfinished piano concerto as part of the score.

In *Petrushka* Stravinsky began to experiment more deeply with novel rhythmic and harmonic effects: for example, using clashing tunes in different keys, played at the same time. Many passages in the score recalled Russian folk songs, but no Russian music had ever sounded quite like this. At the first rehearsal, members of the orchestra actually laughed, thinking the score an unplayable joke. In retrospect, *Petrushka* is one of the seminal works of twentieth-century music.

Petrushka is the sad tale of a puppet with a soul, caught up in a doomed love triangle with his fellow puppets. It represents the best of the Ballets Russes's remarkable spirit of artistic collaboration, and Nijinsky made the pathetic, tormented dancing puppet a figure of high tragedy. It was his greatest role.

After experiencing *Petrushka*, the famous actress Sarah Bernhardt proclaimed Nijinsky "the finest actor in the world." Once in character, in his costume and makeup, he kept his face expressionless and blank, with eyes like black buttons, quizzical eyebrows painted high on his forehead; his arms were held stiffly, his normally expressive hands encased in mittens. A dance critic described his performance: "Nijinsky succeeded in investing the movements of his legs with a looseness suggesting that foot, leg and thigh were threaded on a string attached to the hip . . . his limbs spasmodically leapt or twisted or stamped like the reflex actions of limbs whose muscles have been subjected to an electric current. . . . He suggested a puppet that sometimes aped a human being [instead of] a dancer imitating a puppet. He seemed to have probed the very soul of the character with astonishing intuition. Did he, in one of his dark moods of introspection, feel conscious of a strange parallel between Petrushka and himself, and the showman and Diaghilev?"

After three years together, Nijinsky and Diaghilev had a complex relationship, and Nijinsky was beginning to chafe under Diaghilev's near-total dominance. Although emotionally and professionally connected to the man, he felt no physical attraction. He had become disgusted by the smudges of jet-black hair pomade that Diaghilev left on his pillows, and he mocked the monocle that Diaghilev affected but didn't need. "I used to lock my door," Nijinsky wrote later in life, "because our rooms were next to each other. I did not allow anyone in." They were no longer sexually intimate. A young man in his early twenties, Vatsa was exploring his ambivalent sexuality. It seems clear from his statements and actions throughout his life that although he had two serious, long-lasting homosexual relationships, in the end he was bisexual, equally attracted to women. Nijinsky tried to slip out alone whenever he could to wander around Paris and pick up streetwalkers. "As I was alone, I masturbated and chased tarts. . . . Diaghilev thought I went out for walks, but I was chasing tarts. . . . I knew that what I was doing was horrible. . . . I was very young and so did silly things. . . . I made love to several tarts a day. . . . I did not like what I was doing, but my habits became more complex and I took to looking for them every day." He was absolutely terrified of being recognized, but he was compelled to continue his erotic adventures. Vassili, Nijinsky's dresser and Diaghilev's loyal employee, kept a close eye on Vatsa and reported some of his activities to the boss. The impresario and his star performer were growing apart, and Nijinsky's life was far from happy.

Later in life Nijinsky himself referred to Petrushka as "the mythical outcast in whom is concentrated the pathos and suffering of life, one who beats his hands against the walls, but is always cheated and despised and left outside alone . . . a clown of God." Perhaps his tortured performance was a kind of unconscious self-portrait.

JUNE 13, 1911

THE BALLETS RUSSES

presents

PETRUSHKA

MUSIC BY Igor Stravinsky
CHOREOGRAPHY BY Mikhail Fokine
STORY BY Alexandre Benois and Igor Stravinsky
DESIGN AND COSTUMES BY Alexandre Benois

"The great difficulty of Petrushka's part is to express his pitiful oppression and his hopeless efforts to achieve personal dignity without ceasing to be a puppet."

ALEXANDRE BENOIS, ARTIST, CRITIC, HISTORIAN

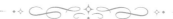

AS PART OF A STREET FAIR'S entertainment, three puppets dance for the crowd—a moor, a ballerina, and Petrushka, a tattered clown. But backstage the puppets have lives of their own. Petrushka is in love with the ballerina, who has eyes only for the moor. In a fit of jealousy, the moor kills Petrushka. The puppeteer appears, revealing that Petrushka is only a puppet. Or so it would appear....

The ballet opened and closed on a crowded street fair, while the second act was set inside Petrushka's claustrophobic storage box. There Nijinsky performed an agonizing solo as Petrushka railed against the puppeteer's cruelty and the hopelessness of his unrequited love. During the third act, the puppets rushed out of their boxes and into the street fair, where the moor killed Petrushka with his scimitar. The fairgoers were horrified until the puppeteer demonstrated that Petrushka was nothing more than a doll filled with straw. But after he was dragged away, Petrushka's spirit appeared, dangling defiantly above the puppet theater as the ballet ended with a strange ironic flourish in the music.

VASLAV NIJINSKY

as Petrushka

The Ballets Russes program for The Afternoon of a Faun,
with a costume sketch by Léon Bakst, 1912

6

The Afternoon of a Faun

AFTER THE 1911 PARIS SEASON, Diaghilev took the Ballets Russes to England to perform at the coronation gala of King George V. The event was attended by dignitaries from all over the British Empire, resplendent in their opulent regalia. Karsavina later recalled that she was dazzled and almost distracted by the reflection of stage lights from the jewels of the audience. The Russian performance was a smash, and Diaghilev and company were feted all over London just as they had been in Paris. By this time the Ballets Russes was an important part of the avant-garde movement in Europe, and the British audiences embraced the troupe in their reserved British way, their polite applause muffled by kid gloves. But the enthusiasm was very real, and a new word came into vogue to describe the phenomenon—*balletomania*.

Nijinsky started planning a ballet of his own during the 1911 season. He was determined to try his hand at choreography, with Diaghilev's support. Until now Diaghilev had relied on Fokine for the company's choreography and perhaps felt that Nijinsky should be groomed as a backup. He was always looking for fresh, new ideas, and undoubtedly he also wanted his friend to explore and fulfill his potential as an artist. Diaghilev suggested the composition *Prelude to the Afternoon of a Faun*, by the French impressionist composer Claude Debussy. The piece is short, lasting only about twelve minutes, and is beautiful, dreamy, and evocative in mood—seemingly perfect for a dancer's first tentative effort at choreography. Little did Diaghilev realize that in one bold stroke Nijinsky would create a rigorous masterpiece that pointed the art of dance in an entirely new direction by breaking all the rules of classical ballet.

Nijinsky began his creative process by looking at ancient art and exploring the faun's roots in Greek mythology. In Paris he visited the Louvre Museum and studied Greek vases, Minoan frescoes, and Egyptian relief sculpture for inspiration. In these forms of art, figures do not move in three dimensions but exist and interact in a narrow band of space. Faces are shown in profile, while shoulders and torsos are shown from the front, with hips and legs once again in profile. This distinctive look became the guiding principle behind Nijinsky's choreography for the piece.

The Afternoon of a Faun was first performed for a select audience in Paris on May 28, 1912, at the Théâtre du Châtelet. The puzzled audience watched respectfully, waiting to be amazed. Expecting their familiar God of Dance with his fantastic grand pirouettes and thrilling leaps, they were disappointed. The ballet did not feature dancing in the then-traditional sense. Nijinsky's fantastic woodland creature—half man, half goat—and the nymphs he encountered basically strode back and forth, making unusual gestures, inter-acting, and occasionally striking poses. Near the end of the ballet, Nijinsky remained onstage alone with a scarf the nymphs had left behind. He took it slowly and deliberately to his rock, caressed it, placed it on the stage, and lay facedown on top of it. In the ballet's final moments, while lying on the nymph's scarf, Nijinsky apparently made a small thrust with his hips—quite the shocking gesture in 1912. The elite audience was stupefied and silent. Indignant but also shrewd, Diaghilev ordered that the entire ballet be repeated, so the first-night audience experienced Nijinsky's Faun twice before enjoying complimentary champagne and caviar in the theater lobby, no doubt lightening their mood. But at the official premiere on May 29, the ballet concluded to boos and jeers as well as cheers.

The next day, reviews brought some praise for the ballet, along with a firestorm of criticism. The stylized yet coolly erotic choreography was simply too radical for many to appreciate. One critic was offended by the half-human, half-animal characterization, and Nijinsky's final move was singled out by several as lewd and base. The controversy over the ballet's final moments only enhanced Nijinsky's already scandalous image, and it didn't hurt at the box office.

Fokine, however, had had enough. Nijinsky's project had initially been developed in secret. When the official rehearsals began, Fokine could be kept in the dark no longer, and he decided that he could not work for Diaghilev alongside a rival choreographer. Mikhail Fokine, official choreographer of the Ballets Russes and creator of most of Nijinsky's greatest roles, resigned at the end of the 1912 season.

Fokine's choreography had been revolutionary in its time, but *The Afternoon of a Faun* ushered in a new era of modern dance and is now considered a masterpiece. With his debut as choreographer, Nijinsky emphatically rejected the past and pointed a way to the future. He was already hard at work on two new ballets.

MAY 29, 1912

THE BALLETS RUSSES

presents

THE AFTERNOON OF A FAUN

MUSIC BY Claude Debussy

STORY AND CHOREOGRAPHY BY Vaslav Nijinsky

DESIGN AND COSTUMES BY Léon Bakst

"Nijinsky has never been so remarkable as in his latest role."

AUGUSTE RODIN, SCULPTOR

A YOUNG FAUN encounters a group of nymphs, becoming increasingly aggressive until the nymphs disappear, leaving behind a scarf.

As choreographer, Nijinsky refined every movement of *The Afternoon of a Faun* and allowed no deviation from his concept. Unable to articulate his vision, Nijinsky explained his ideas by demonstrating them. He required his dancers to put aside their classical technique, assume new and awkward positions, and make precise, difficult movements. Nijinsky needed more than ninety rehearsals before he was satisfied. The result was spare, severe, strangely erotic, totally orig- inal, and very beautiful. The dancers went back and forth from pose to pose, their faces in strict profile, their hands slicing the air. The nymphs wore gauzy gowns in the style of ancient Greece, and Nijinsky's tights were painted with brown patches resembling a pony's hide. He wore a head- dress of golden horns and sported pointed ears of wax and a tiny goat's tail. The unconventional ballet stirred controversy, with audiences both praising and con- demning Nijinsky's erotic choreography.

BRONISLAVA NIJINSKA *as a nymph*
& VASLAV NIJINSKY *as the Faun*

Costume sketch for The Rite of Spring
by Nicholas Roerich, 1912

Games and Rituals

WITH FOKINE GONE, Nijinsky spent the autumn and winter of 1912 working on the 1913 season. His second ballet was inspired by a tennis match he had seen in England. He titled it *Jeux* (French for "games"). Diaghilev approached Debussy to write the score, but the famous composer declined. He had not been happy with either the choreography or the controversy surrounding *The Afternoon of a Faun*. But when Diaghilev offered to double his fee, Debussy decided to accept the commission.

Nijinsky choreographed *Jeux* as an extended pas de trois with himself and two ballerinas (one of whom was Karsavina). Again he broke new ground: for the first time, here was a ballet about contemporary people. Nijinsky's choreography once again required his dancers to suppress their training and make unusual, uncomfortable movements. Even his good friend Karsavina complained at rehearsals. *Jeux* was not well received, unfortunately. It had only a few performances, and today the choreography is completely lost. All that remains of Nijinsky's second ballet are some verbal descriptions, some painted sketches, Debussy's score, and a few photographs.

Jeux was quickly overshadowed by the impact of Nijinsky's next ballet, which premiered two weeks later. Before he'd started composing *Petrushka*, Igor Stravinsky had begun preliminary musical sketches for another big ballet. He claimed that the idea had come to him in "a fleeting vision. . . . I saw in imagination a solemn pagan rite: sage elders, seated in a circle, watched a young girl dance. . . . They were sacrificing her to . . . the god of spring." Stravinsky conferred with Nicholas Roerich, an artist, anthropologist, and expert on ancient Russia. He had painted the backdrop for "Polovtsian Dances" in 1909. Together Stravinsky and Roerich created a scenario for the ballet. When they presented their idea to Diaghilev, he was at first annoyed that they had not consulted him in advance, but he quickly came around. After all, he had struck gold with Stravinsky twice before, and this new concept would be Nijinsky's first ballet spectacle with an elaborate production involving the entire company.

Roerich was engaged to design the scenery and costumes. At this point they called the ballet *The Great Sacrifice*, but eventually it was retitled *Holy Spring* in Russian. This translated into French as *Le Sacre du Printemps*, which became in English *The Rite of Spring*.

Nijinsky choreographed the part of the Sacrificial Maiden specifically for his sister, Bronislava. But she had recently married, and during the creative process she became pregnant and had to withdraw from the role. Her brother was highly annoyed and disappointed. He had to teach the choreography to her replacement, a young dancer named Maria Piltz. From eyewitness accounts, Nijinsky's own performance of the "Sacrificial Dance" while teaching the part was an intensely moving experience.

The Rite of Spring was first performed on May 29, 1913, at the Théâtre des Champs-Elysées. The theater was brand-new, having opened only about two months before. Nijinsky by now was so celebrated that his image was included in the sculptural decoration on the facade of the new building. Although tickets were double priced, the box office was sold out and the theater packed. Little did the theatergoers know that they would have their own part to play in one of the most infamous events in theatrical history.

The evening began serenely enough with *Les Sylphides*, the most traditional ballet in the Ballets Russes's repertoire. Nijinsky, in the role of a romantic poet, was charmed and inspired by a stage full of ballerinas in long tutus, set to the romantic music of Frédéric Chopin. With Karsavina as leading ballerina, *Les Sylphides* was a familiar crowd-pleaser that was meant to lull the audience and set it up for the shock of what was to follow after the interval.

The Rite of Spring begins with a strange, plaintive melody played by the bassoon in the thin tones of its highest register. From the first notes the audience was restless, wary of the unfamiliar sounds from the orchestra. A few minutes in, when the curtain was raised and the actual dancing began, there were catcalls and jeers. Soon the pounding rhythms, clashing chords, and unconventional, awkward moves of the choreography had divided the audience into two factions, pro and con. The dancers were working hard and sweating profusely in the heat of the stage lights under their wigs, false beards, and heavy wool caps, tunics, and leggings. As the audience grew more raucous, the dancers could not hear the music. At one point, Stravinsky, alarmed and appalled by the audience's reaction, rushed backstage to find Nijinsky standing on a chair in the wings drenched in sweat, his face dead-white, pumping both fists to beat out the rhythm while frantically screaming out—"*Ras, dva, tri!*" (One, two, three!) over the din to his dancers. Eventually there was a full-scale riot in the theater. People hurled insults at one another and threw their programs at the orchestra. There were even a few fistfights between the opposing factions. Diaghilev ordered the houselights raised, and the police were called to help restore order.

Throughout the melee the conductor somehow kept the orchestra together, and the dancers, with Nijinsky's shouted instructions, were able to bring the work to conclusion. It must have been a wrenching and utterly exhausting experience for Nijinsky, who then had to make up his face, change into costume, have his rose petals sewn on, and compose himself to perform *The Specter of the Rose* with Karsavina.

Afterward, while excitedly rehashing the premiere with Stravinsky and Nijinsky and some hangers-on, Diaghilev expressed great pleasure at the outcome, saying, "Exactly what I wanted." The *succès de scandale* of an actual brawl in the theater was the best publicity he could imagine. But the next day most critics were brutal. One newspaper riffed on the French title, calling the ballet *Le MASSacre du Printemps*. The great Italian opera composer Giacomo Puccini recorded his impression of the music as "the work of a madman."

But the naysayers were proven wrong. They were used to gorgeous, hyperromantic music in which lush harmonies and ravishing melody are the hallmarks. Stravinsky's innovation was to emphasize rhythm as the driving force behind the music; it seemed raw and primitive, just as it was meant to. The score would become a touchstone for modern music.

Stravinsky's ballet music has an immediate visceral power and was performed for a large and influential public. After three masterpieces in a row, each greater than the last, Igor Stravinsky found himself the most famous young composer in the world. And after the riot at the first performance, Nijinsky's provocative reputation was also ratcheted up yet another notch. In retrospect the premiere of *The Rite of Spring* has been regarded by music critics as the most important event in the history of twentieth-century music.

The Rite of Spring was performed a total of nine times during the 1913 season in Paris and London. There were no more riots, but the ballet's controversial reputation had already been made, and each new audience struggled to understand what they were experiencing. With their shockingly original music and choreography, Stravinsky and Nijinsky had positioned the Ballets Russes squarely in the vanguard of the international artistic movement called modernism. Today *The Rite of Spring* is celebrated in the words of one dance historian as "a twentieth-century icon, a summation of modernism at its most subversive and visionary."

But in spite of the artistic value of *The Rite of Spring*, *Jeux*, and *The Afternoon of a Faun*, Nijinsky's choreography was too radical for many to accept. He was a purist, idealistically following his muse. Diaghilev was at first enthusiastic about Nijinsky's choreography, but in the end he was a businessman. Disappointed by the critical and popular reception of the ballets, he made the decision to end Nijinsky's choreographic experiments, at least for the moment. The cracks in their relationship had opened wide. Nijinsky wrote, "I began to hate him quite openly and once pushed him on a street in Paris . . . to show him that I was not afraid of him. Diaghilev hit me with a stick." A Nijinsky biographer wrote that the dancer ran away in tears, "with the great, lumbering Diaghilev chasing after him." In the late summer of 1913, the two men were at a crossroads.

THE BALLETS RUSSES

presents

JEUX

MUSIC BY Claude Debussy

STORY AND CHOREOGRAPHY BY Vaslav Nijinsky

DESIGN AND COSTUMES BY Léon Bakst

"Before I composed a ballet I didn't know what a choreographer was. Now I know — he is a very strong and mathematical gentleman."

CLAUDE DEBUSSY, COMPOSER

IN A GARDEN AT DUSK, a boy and two girls play erotic games as they search for a missing tennis ball. They are interrupted and alarmed when another tennis ball is thrown into the garden, and they disappear into the darkness.

Jeux was the first ballet with dancers as contemporary characters, as well as the first ballet inspired by sport. The costumes were white flannel versions of ballet rehearsal clothes, and the set was illuminated by large electric lamps. Nijinsky originally wanted the ballet to end with an airplane crashing onstage, but this proved too difficult to execute. *Jeux* was an abstract ballet in which the dancers moved from pose to pose, coupling and uncoupling in different combinations. Later in life, Nijinsky revealed that the ballet was inspired by Diaghilev's desire to make love with two men at the same time. Nijinsky made two of the dancers girls, since an erotic relationship between three men onstage would have been too shocking for the times, even for sophisticated Parisian audiences.

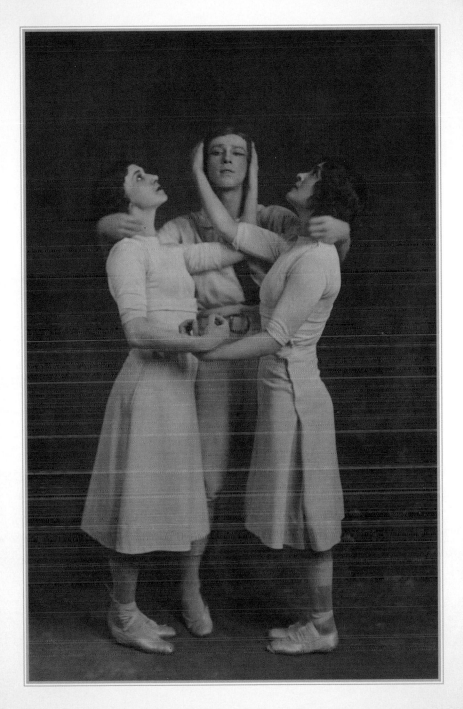

VASLAV NIJINSKY *as the Boy*

TAMARA KARSAVINA & LUDMILLA SCHOLLAR *as the Girls*

THE BALLETS RUSSES

presents

THE RITE OF SPRING

MUSIC BY Igor Stravinsky
CHOREOGRAPHY BY Vaslav Nijinsky
STORY BY Igor Stravinsky and Nicholas Roerich
DESIGN AND COSTUMES BY Nicholas Roerich

"This is a biological ballet . . . not the usual spring sung by poets, with its breezes, its birdsong, its pale skies and tender greens. Here is nothing but the harsh struggle of growth, the panic terror of the rising of the sap. . . . Spring seen from inside, with its violence, its spasms and its fissions. We seem to be watching a drama through a microscope."

JACQUES RIVIÈRE, WRITER, CRITIC, AND EDITOR

A PREHISTORIC RUSSIAN TRIBE performs sacred rituals in honor of the coming spring. The tribal elders choose a young woman to be sacrificed.

In *The Rite of Spring*, Stravinsky composed a revolutionary score so audacious and original, so brutal and harsh, that when combined with Nijinsky's unconventional choreography, it caused the audience to riot. Inspired by traditional Russian folk tunes, Stravinsky fragmented and layered his score in a musical process similar to the techniques that Picasso used in his cubist paintings. There was no grace or beauty in Nijinsky's choreography, and his dancers balked at his demands. As part of an anonymous crowd, the dancers plodded in procession, shuffled in circles, stamped their feet, lunged, twirled, and jumped up and down. At the ballet's end, the maiden chosen as a sacrifice was not merely killed. Instead, she was forced to dance to clashing, savage, disturbingly violent music. Gripped by the relentless, spasmodic driving rhythm and in a frenzy of awe and terror, she danced herself . . . to death!

SERGEI DIAGHILEV & IGOR STRAVINSKY

Nijinsky and his wife, Romola de Pulszky, 1916

Romola

AT THE AGE OF TWENTY-FOUR, Nijinsky was no longer the callow youth Diaghilev had first met and championed. He was now a grown man, the world-famous God of Dance—a major artist and celebrated star of the Ballets Russes. It was perhaps inevitable that he would rebel against Diaghilev's control, though when he finally did, it was in an astonishing way.

After the 1913 Paris and London seasons, the Ballets Russes was booked to tour South America, and in mid-August the company set sail on the SS *Avon*. Diaghilev was terrified of ocean travel. He had once been told by a fortune-teller that he would die at sea, and so he elected not to go on the tour. For the first time in his adult life, Nijinsky was far away from Diaghilev for an extended period. The past few years had been increasingly difficult, with the strains of mounting his own ballets weighing heavily upon Nijinsky and Diaghilev constantly monitoring his protégé's every move. It was a relief to relax into the comfortable routine of an extended ocean voyage. He even took his daily ballet class on deck in the open air where the other passengers could watch.

Another passenger on the *Avon* was Romola de Pulszky, a pampered society girl from Budapest and the daughter of Emília Márkus, Hungary's leading actress. Her father had been a prominent politician but had committed suicide when she was a child. Romola was twenty-two years old, attractive, spoiled, headstrong, conniving, and relentless, and she had become fixated upon Nijinsky. She'd seen him first as Harlequin in *Carnaval* and traveled to attend every performance that she could. She was engaged to be married but broke it off to pursue Nijinsky.

Over a period of months, she had wormed her way into the fringes of the Ballets Russes, first as a groupie, then by pretending to have a burning desire to dance. She persuaded Diaghilev to hire her as a second-string dancer despite her inexperience and lack of technique, probably because he was impressed by her mother's fame and social connections. More sophisticated than the career dancers, she dressed well, traveled with her personal maid, and actually smoked cigarettes—very risqué for a young woman in 1913.

During the voyage, Romola turned up wherever Nijinsky was. Gradually he became aware of her attention—she made herself hard to miss—and at first he pointedly ignored her. But when she finally arranged a formal introduction, she managed to convince Nijinsky of her love of ballet, even though they could communicate only in halting, basic French. Even after that, although politely cordial, he still paid very little attention to her for the rest of the trip.

But as the voyage neared its end, out of the blue Nijinsky sent word by a third party to Romola that he wanted to marry her! At first she thought it a cruel joke, but she agreed to meet with him. He proposed by pointing to his ring finger and asking, *"Mademoiselle, voulez-vous, vous et moi?"* Her answer was *"Oui, oui, oui!"* When they docked in Buenos Aires, a wedding was quickly arranged, and suddenly Vaslav Nijinsky was a married man. It was an astounding, even mind-boggling move. Nijinsky and his bride had spoken only a few times, had no language in common, and had never spent time alone together. They were virtually strangers.

The traveling ballet company was dumbfounded. Several of the dancers had tried to discourage Romola's advances since Nijinsky's relationship with Diaghilev was common knowledge. Bronia and her mother learned of the marriage from the newspapers, before Nijinsky's telegram had arrived. They were aghast. His sister would never forgive Romola's intrusion into her Vatsa's life. When Diaghilev received Nijinsky's telegram, he was thunderstruck and "overcome by a sort of hysteria . . . sobbing and shouting." Stravinsky recalled, "I watched him turn into a madman." Diaghilev immediately cabled South America to see if he could intervene, but it was too late. He felt duped and humiliated. By turns both livid and grief-stricken, he had been totally blindsided, and after the initial shock, he was consumed by a black rage and vowed revenge. Then he "gave himself to a wild orgy of dissipation."

The newlyweds began their married life awkwardly. Because of the language barrier, they could scarcely communicate. At the end of their wedding day, Nijinsky bid his wife a rather formal good night, kissed her hand, and retired to his own hotel room, leaving Romola alone and confused, but also relieved. Like most well-brought-up young women of her era, she knew little about sex and had been apprehensive about her wedding night. The next morning, she awakened to a fresh bouquet of white roses from her husband. After that, things must have warmed up between them quickly, for by the time the company sailed back to Europe, Romola Nijinsky was pregnant. The young couple immediately traveled to Budapest so that Nijinsky might meet Emília Márkus, his new mother-in-law.

Nijinsky apparently thought—naïvely—that Diaghilev would simply accept his new life and their professional relationship would go on as before.

When it was clear that would be impossible, Nijinsky asked Stravinsky to use his influence with Diaghilev to intervene. But at this point Diaghilev got his revenge. He summarily fired Nijinsky from the Ballets Russes. Wasting no time, Diaghilev had discovered a new protégé to groom for stardom: an eighteen-year-old actor and dancer named Léonide Massine. Mikhail Fokine was welcomed back as choreographer of the Ballets Russes, under the condition that he himself would dance Nijinsky's roles and that Nijinsky's own ballets would be shelved. Nijinsky's original choreography for *The Rite of Spring* would never be seen again. It may have been his greatest masterpiece. We shall never know.

Nijinsky now had a wife and a child on the way. He was a famous artist, but he had no job, no place to live, and since he was liable for military service if he returned to Russia, no homeland. He also had very little money. As Diaghilev's companion, he'd had no contract and had taken no salary. Romola had expected to live a life of luxury as the spouse of a rich celebrity. One dance critic states that her life's ambition "was to wear furs and lunch with duchesses." For his part, Nijinsky may have assumed she was a wealthy heiress, but Romola had no real money of her own either. Her relationship with her mother was strained, and Emília Márkus had no intention of supporting the newlyweds.

Under these conditions, Nijinsky felt forced to accept an offer from London to organize a dance troupe and perform for eight weeks during March and April 1914 at the Palace Theatre, a popular vaudeville music hall. Performing in this kind of theater along with other types of entertainment was a prospect that the great Nijinsky viewed with withering contempt, in spite of, or maybe because of, the fact that it was precisely what his parents had done, albeit on a larger scale. But he desperately needed the money, and so he signed a contract. Bronia and her husband came to help organize things, and soon Nijinsky found himself dancing, as he said, "sandwiched between performing dogs and acrobats."

The situation was an absolute disaster. Bronia resented Romola, who was jealous of the close bond between brother and sister. Nijinsky had zero administrative skills for organizing a company, and his normal, reasonable artistic demands were ignored. The unsophisticated music-hall audiences had no appreciation of his art, and ballet lovers who came to see him were disappointed with his performances in the raucous music-hall environment. Away from the hothouse atmosphere of the Ballets Russes and the protection of Diaghilev, and after all the recent upheaval, some of the old magic was gone.

After a few backstage screaming tantrums and missed performances, his contract was canceled, and the Nijinskys dejectedly went to Vienna. There, in June 1914, Romola gave birth to a daughter. They named her Kyra. She had her father's features, and he doted on her. Vaslav Nijinsky turned out to be a wonderful, loving father, but otherwise it was the beginning of a dreadful time. Only nine days after Kyra's birth, Archduke Franz Ferdinand of Austria-Hungary was assassinated, and Europe careened headlong into war. As months passed and the war escalated, Nijinsky found himself in a desperate position. As a Russian, he was considered an enemy combatant and placed under house arrest, confined to Budapest and the Márkus home. Already an artist in exile, the God of Dance was now a prisoner of war.

*Nijinsky applying a dancer's makeup before
a performance of* Till Eulenspiegel, *1916*

The War Years

NIJINSKY WAS TRAPPED IN HUNGARY in the household of a hostile mother-in-law. She resented his presence and tried to persuade Romola to divorce him. His wife was sometimes loving and supportive, but at other times she was selfish, self-absorbed, and critical, disappointed that her plans for a life of luxury had been dashed. The servants were suspicious of Nijinsky's Russian origins and considered him one of the enemy. For the first time since childhood, Nijinsky was not dancing, and he was devastated by the inactivity. It was difficult even to continue his daily exercises at the barre.

For a year and a half, Nijinsky endured these stifling conditions. He worked restlessly on various projects, such as inventing a way to choreograph on paper with symbols, much like musical notation, so that a dance could be preserved and reproduced. (At first, the servants suspected he was working on a secret spy code.) He also worked on several ideas for ballets. He wanted to choreograph a dance to the music of J. S. Bach. He had an idea for a

Japanese ballet, and another for a ballet about life in a brothel. He already had the music for a ballet about Till Eulenspiegel, a sort of medieval Robin Hood figure—a merry jester who plays jokes on pompous people, exposing their pretensions, and who comes to a bad end. German composer Richard Strauss had composed a tone poem about the character that Nijinsky used as his inspiration. But, for now, confined to Budapest, he could only plan and dream. And underlying all of this was Nijinsky's horror at the senseless waste and slaughter of the war. The only real joy in his life was his daughter.

Then suddenly, there came a reprieve. Since many European venues were closed due to the war, a financially strapped Diaghilev arranged to send the Ballets Russes to New York for a season and then on an extended tour of America. His sponsor was the Metropolitan Opera Company, and they demanded that the world-famous Nijinsky be part of the package. Diaghilev had moved on by now, and with his anger spent and an eye on the box office, he called in every favor to get Nijinsky and his family out of confinement. The king of Spain and even the pope were involved. After months of negotiation, passports were finally produced, and in April 1916 the Nijinskys made their way to New York, where they were met by Diaghilev, who had apparently overcome his fear of ocean travel. Right away Romola stirred the pot by making new financial demands, but Diaghilev needed Nijinsky, so they negotiated a settlement.

Then Diaghilev departed for Europe, unfortunately and inexplicably leaving Nijinsky, with his lack of administrative and communication skills, in charge of the traveling company. But before he left, Diaghilev approved the Till Eulenspiegel idea, with Strauss's tone poem as the score, and so Nijinsky was a choreographer once more. A young American artist, Robert Edmond Jones, was hired to design sets and costumes. He worked with Nijinsky during the summer of 1916 and described his impressions of the dancer: "He is very nervous. His eyes are troubled. . . . He seems tired, bored, excited, all at once." There is "an impression of something too eager, too brilliant, a quiver of the nerves, a nature racked to dislocation by a merciless creative urge." That autumn, *Till Eulenspiegel* was presented in New York to rave reviews.

After the New York season, the company embarked on a four-month tour across America. It must have been very strange for the Russians, after years of glamorous and glittering evenings in sophisticated European capitals, to be playing in small cities to provincial audiences who had no real understanding of what they were seeing. In the South, people were particularly outraged by *Scheherazade*. Nijinsky's sexy Golden Slave was singled out in a racist statement by a critic as a repulsive "Negro who makes love to the princess" and deserved a thrashing.

In Los Angeles Nijinsky met Charlie Chaplin, the iconic silent movie star from the early days of cinema. These two great artists hit it off immediately. After their meeting, Chaplin wrote of Nijinsky, "The moment he appeared I was electrified. I have seen few geniuses in this world, and Nijinsky was one of them. He was hypnotic, god-like, his somberness suggesting moods of other worlds; every movement was poetry, every leap a flight into strange fancy."

Nijinsky and Chaplin had much in common. They were the same age and had grown up backstage as children of entertainers. Both were gifted artists who acted brilliantly without speaking, and each practiced his respective art at the highest level. There are even affinities between Chaplin's immortal character the Tramp and Nijinsky's Petrushka. One was comic and the other tragic, but both were filled with genuine pathos. But there was one fundamental difference between the two young artists. When they met in 1917, Nijinsky's career was nearly done, while Chaplin's was skyrocketing. In spite of his great fame, Nijinsky's audience was only those thousands of people who saw him perform live, while Chaplin's audience was the millions who saw him on-screen. For the first time in history, technology made it possible to reach a mass audience, resulting in an entirely new level of fame. By the early 1920s, Charlie Chaplin was arguably the most famous person on earth.

Nijinsky with Charlie Chaplin on set in Los Angeles, 1917

The New York season had been successful, and the Nijinskys enjoyed their time there, but overall the American tour was a colossal failure. Nijinsky was a wretched administrator, and his arrogance and pompous attitude irritated the dancers. He became morose and withdrawn, and morale in the company sank. The Metropolitan Opera Company lost a quarter of a million dollars, and in the end, Diaghilev's hopes for a financial windfall were crushed. By the time the company returned to Europe, Diaghilev had organized another South American tour to generate money. An exhausted Nijinsky didn't want to go, but he had made a verbal commitment, and Diaghilev forced his hand by threatening legal action.

During this tour Nijinsky's mood darkened even more. Romola convinced him that someone was trying to harm him after he was nearly injured by a few scenery and staging problems. A paranoid Nijinsky began to dread performing, but contractually he had no choice. He was the star of the show, but it was clear that Diaghilev was merely using him to draw audiences. Dejected once more, Nijinsky and Romola returned to Europe in late 1917. With the extra proceeds that Romola had negotiated, they moved into a villa in the charming village of St. Moritz, in Switzerland. Nijinsky knew that he would never dance for Diaghilev again. What he could not know was that his professional career was over. Nijinsky's last appearance before a paying audience had been in South America.

OCTOBER 23, 1916

THE BALLETS RUSSES

presents

TILL EULENSPIEGEL

MUSIC AND STORY BY Richard Strauss

CHOREOGRAPHY BY Vaslav Nijinsky

DESIGN AND COSTUMES BY Robert Edmond Jones

"Mr. Nijinsky has furnished abundant proof of his genius as a stage director. There is almost none of what the average audience would call 'dancing.' . . . Instead, the members of the company have been drilled in strange posturings and queer little movements that . . . remind you that you are in the midst of a medieval fantasy."

NEW YORK TIMES, OCTOBER 24, 1916

A MEDIEVAL JESTER has a series of adventures at the expense of rich townsfolk — causing mayhem, stirring rebellion, and making people look like fools. Though he is brought to justice and executed, his spirit lives on.

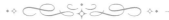

Nijinsky based his choreography on the preexisting story written into Strauss's music. The designer provided elaborately skewed sets and bizarre costumes in a highly exaggerated medieval style.

Nijinsky's choreography has been lost, unfortunately. The only impression of its qualities comes from out-of-focus photographs of him posing in costume.

The ballet received rave reviews at its New York premiere, but Nijinsky hadn't completed the choreography and wasn't satisfied with the result. Parts of the crowd scenes had to be improvised, which wasn't Nijinsky's usual method. *Till Eulenspiegel* was never produced again and was the only Ballets Russes production not presented in Europe. Diaghilev never saw it.

VASLAV NIJINSKY

as Till Eulenspiegel

Nijinsky and his daughter, Kyra, 1916

10

The Last Dance

WITH THE RUSSIAN REVOLUTION OF 1917, the brutal assassination of the czar and his family by the Bolsheviks, and the establishment of a Communist regime, the Russia that Nijinsky had once known no longer existed. He was frantic with worry about Bronia, her family, and his mother, but he was relieved to hear in early 1918 that they all were safe in Kiev.

By this time Nijinsky was settled nicely into the villa in St. Moritz, the only real home he ever had. Switzerland was an idyllic place to live, beautiful and civilized. He practiced his exercises daily on a balcony of the villa. Vatsa and Romola went skating. He carved toys for Kyra, painted her nursery with colorful Russian designs, and took his wife and daughter on sleigh rides. For the first time in his life, he led a somewhat normal day-to-day existence, but in fact, he never had been an ordinary person, and not practicing his art began to take its toll.

Toward the end of 1918, Nijinsky began to behave very strangely. Usually mild mannered and polite in social situations, he now was often argumentative and belligerent. He took to wearing an enormous crucifix around his neck and confronting people in the village. He became reckless while driving the sleigh, and once he pushed Romola down a flight of stairs while she was holding Kyra. Ominously, Nijinsky began to hallucinate, once imagining trails of blood splattered in the snow when there was nothing there. He spent hours compulsively drawing—page after page of intersecting circles that resembled huge staring eyes or bizarre masks. When Romola asked about these images, he said that they were the faces of dead soldiers. Clearly the horrors of the Great War had affected him deeply. Despite all this, and even though Bronia sent the sad news that their brother, Stassik, had died, Christmas that year in St. Moritz was a relatively happy one for Nijinsky and his family. It would be their last happy time together.

Early in January 1919, Nijinsky decided to give a private dance recital in the village. A hall was booked, invitations were sent, and a friend agreed to play the piano. Nijinsky declared to his wife that he would improvise a new ballet onstage at the recital. Romola was apprehensive. On January 19, 1919, Nijinsky began his recital by straddling a chair and staring intently at the audience of about two hundred people without moving. As the long minutes passed, it became excruciating. Finally an alarmed Romola took the initiative and prompted the pianist to begin playing. The intense staring spell was broken. Nijinsky performed some virtuoso turns to the music of Chopin and then unfurled some bolts of velvet fabric on the floor in the form of a cross. He stood at the head of the fabric cross with his arms held out, forming another cross, and declared, "Now I will dance you the war, with its suffering, with its destruction, with its death." A member of the audience described the dance in detail:

And we saw Nijinsky, his face ravaged with fright and horror, walking to the sound of a funeral march on a field of battle, striding over a rotting corpse, avoiding a shell, defending a shallow trench which was soaked in blood that clung to his feet, attacking an enemy, running from a tank, coming back on his steps, wounded, dying, tearing, with hands that spoke volumes, the clothes which covered him and were now becoming rags and tatters. Nijinsky, barely covered with the shreds of his tunic and gasping for breath, was panting hard. A feeling of oppression came over the room. . . . One last spasm shook his body which seems riddled with bullets. . . . We felt too much overwhelmed to applaud. We were looking at a pitiful corpse and our silence was the silence that enfolds the dead.

Nijinsky's dance recital was a powerful piece of performance art, improvised in the moment. It was a harrowing experience for the audience and undoubtedly for Nijinsky as well. His tragic depiction of the horrors of war had been wrenched from the depths of his troubled soul. It was his swan song. The great Nijinsky would never dance in public again.

Romola now knew for certain that he was spiraling out of control. Already alarmed by his recent strange behavior, she had begun consulting with doctors behind his back. After his recital, she feared that her husband was losing his mind.

A drawing by Nijinsky, 1918

11

A Leap into Madness

ON THE VERY DAY OF HIS RECITAL, Nijinsky began keeping a journal. *The Diary of Vaslav Nijinsky* is less a diary and more a searing personal account of an artistic genius's futile struggle with extreme mental illness. It is an astonishing and unique document. Nijinsky writes in a passionate stream of consciousness about Diaghilev, Romola, his troubled sexuality, his talent, his art, his fame, his bodily functions, politics, religion, and God. Sometimes his words are lucid and perceptive, sometimes unintelligible and absurd. The writing is strange and disjointed, his thoughts lurching from subject to subject. For six weeks he wrote compulsively, knowing that something was horribly wrong, trying desperately to understand what was happening, and striving to claw his way back to reality. He knew he was being watched and evaluated by medical professionals. When questioned, he even claimed to be acting the part of a madman as a demonstration of his genius! But he became more and more difficult and irrational as he sank irrevocably into madness.

In his journal he reveals a long-simmering, guilt-ridden disgust with sex and exhibits delusions of grandeur as he comes to embrace his despair as a merging with a higher consciousness. The God of Dance ends one segment of his journal with these words: "I want to weep, but God commands me to write. . . . God is within me, and I am within him. I want Him. I seek Him. . . . I am a seeker, for I feel God. God is seeking me, and therefore we are finding each other."—signed, "God Nijinsky."

He stopped writing only when Romola and her mother had him committed to an asylum. When the doctor in charge pronounced him schizophrenic and uncurable, Vatsa declared to Romola, "Wife, you are bringing me my death warrant." Vaslav Nijinsky was thirty years old. His life was only half over.

In the beginning, Nijinsky's condition fluctuated as the doctors tried to figure out how to treat him. There were periods of relative lucidity followed by periods of complete delusion, and he was in and out of the asylum. In June 1920, a little more than a year after he was first institutionalized, Romola gave birth to a second daughter, named Tamara. The baby would have been conceived on one of the occasions when Nijinsky was home from the asylum, but here things get murky.

Around the time of Nijinsky's breakdown, Romola apparently began an affair with one of the doctors she had engaged to evaluate him. When Tamara was born, Romola didn't formally acknowledge the child and shipped her off to be raised by her mother, Emília, in Budapest. The doctor himself became addicted to morphine and eventually attempted suicide over the affair. The question of Tamara Nijinsky's paternity has never been completely resolved, and it is certainly possible that Romola herself was not completely sure which man was the father.

Gradually it became clear that Nijinsky's condition was permanent. For the next two decades, he alternated between episodes of inactivity and sudden bursts of manic behavior. For weeks at a time he would sit motionless and nearly mute, only snarling "Do not touch me!" in French if someone came near. At other times he became enraged and dangerously violent, screaming, throwing food or even excrement, smashing furniture, or physically threatening his attendants. Nijinsky was quite strong, and the threat to himself and others was real. Sometimes he injured himself, punching his head or stomach with his fists, biting his hands and arms, or tearing out clumps of his hair. He would make contorted facial grimaces and roll his eyes, or crawl around on all fours and defecate on the floor. Sometimes he masturbated openly or made lewd sexual advances to his attendants. He was more than disturbed—he was profoundly ill, what some would term stark raving mad.

In an era when mental illness was considered shameful and there were virtually no useful treatments, asylums resembled prisons. Nijinsky was subjected over and over to an experimental therapy that one of his doctors had devised. A dance scholar wrote that after an overdose of insulin was injected, Nijinsky "would go into deep shock, sweat, drool, turn blue in the face, convulse violently, and then lapse into a coma for several hours, after which he would be revived by a sugar solution." Over time he had a total of 228 of these treatments. This barbaric insulin shock therapy undoubtedly made things worse. Today we know that it probably damaged his brain, heart, and kidneys. But Romola insisted that the so-called therapy continue. From time to time she would bring Nijinsky home, but by many accounts it seemed that she was too vain or too oblivious to care properly for him. Inevitably he became impossible to handle, and she would confine him once more.

When his sister, Bronia, and his aging mother finally were able to leave Russia in 1921, they spent six weeks traveling by freight train to visit Nijinsky. Bronia sadly wrote, "When we entered his room Vaslav was sitting in an armchair; he did not get up to greet us. Mother rushed to embrace him, but Vaslav showed no emotional reaction. . . . He remained withdrawn into himself, also, when I embraced him. Throughout our visit . . . he had an absent look, staring into space and not uttering a word." Bronia and Eleonora were crushed by the reality of his wretched condition—Vatsa had ended up in an asylum like his poor brother, Stassik.

During one of Nijinsky's docile periods, Diaghilev took him to a performance of *Petrushka*. The tragic puppet was danced by Serge Lifar, a new protégé of Diaghilev's, and Tamara Karsavina was the Ballerina. Nijinsky was totally nonresponsive to the ballet. Afterward he was taken backstage and a famous photograph was made. Diaghilev hovers protectively, Karsavina leans in, trying to engage him, and Nijinsky has a strained smile, though his eyes are staring out at nothing. Later Karsavina said that she thought that her old friend and colleague had perhaps a glimmer of recognition, but she could not be sure.

Over time, even though her husband was alive, Romola assumed the role of a kind of professional widow, trading on his name and his fame to raise money to live on and to support his care. She wrote two books about his life, in which she played fast and loose with the truth. She published a heavily edited version of his journal, carefully rearranging and altering it to put herself in a more positive light. These efforts, while ethically suspect, kept Nijinsky's name in front of the public and achieved their financial purpose.

During the 1930s, Romola spent more and more time away, living her own life. As she grew older, she had a few lesbian relationships. Sometimes several years would pass without her seeing her husband, but she eventually reappeared—her own identity depended upon his reputation and celebrity.

At last the alarming, violent episodes tapered off, and by the 1940s the great Nijinsky had become an unstable, mentally ill middle-aged man, short, balding, and pudgy, his dancer's muscles gone to flab, alternating between living with his wife and returning to the asylum when she tired of caring for him or wanted to travel.

During World War II he was almost killed twice. Once, while he was staying with Romola, a shell exploded near their house. She found him in his room covered in debris, the roof having been blown away. On another occasion, when he had been living in the asylum, someone knocked on Romola's door. An orderly stood there with Nijinsky. He had been smuggled out because the Nazis had given orders to round up the mentally ill as part of "the Final Solution," the German Third Reich's euphemism for the systematic, mechanized murder of anyone deemed undesirable—primarily the Jewish population, but also including Roma people, homosexuals, and the mentally ill. Millions of innocent people were banished to concentration camps and killed. Nijinsky escaped this terrible fate only because of his celebrity.

Later, as the war was ending and the Russian army came through, a troop of soldiers met Nijinsky, whose reputation they knew even though he had not danced in his native country since 1911. Hearing Russian spoken for the first time in many years, he rallied a little, made some halting conversation, and, amazingly, danced a few steps for them.

After the war ended, in 1945, Romola took Nijinsky to England to live. Very occasionally she took him out in public, but he never regained his sanity. In some photographs from this time, his eyes appear unfocused and vacant and he smiles strangely, while in others his eyes are sharp and his face like a mask.

In 1950, at the age of sixty-one and after more than thirty years of illness, Vaslav Nijinsky died peacefully of kidney failure in London and was buried there. A few years later, Serge Lifar arranged for his remains to be taken to Paris, the city of his greatest triumphs, and his coffin was reburied in the cemetery of Montmartre. A heartrending and very fitting monument was erected over the tomb: a life-size bronze figure of Petrushka sits upon Nijinsky's gravestone.

Painting of Nijinsky as the Blue God

Epilogue

Legacy and Legend

*Ten years growing; ten years learning; ten years dancing;
thirty years in eclipse.*

—Richard Buckle, author of
Nijinsky: A Life of Genius and Madness

NIJINSKY'S ACTIVE CAREER as the star of the Ballets Russes lasted for only five years, and all that is left behind of his artistic achievements are some verbal descriptions of his dancing, the music to which he danced, his choreography for *The Afternoon of a Faun* (as remembered by his sister, Bronislava, some years after the fact), a few costumes that were preserved, and a small array of photographs. But we also have his journal, an invaluable and unique window into the troubled mind and heart of a great artist on the brink of insanity.

There are no movies of Nijinsky dancing. During his career the era of motion pictures was in its infancy, and Diaghilev famously allowed no one to film the Ballets Russes's productions. In any case, the relatively primitive film technology of the time would have captured very little of the real effect of a performance onstage. In recent years there have surfaced online a few tantalizing short snippets of film, mere seconds long, jerky and murky, of Nijinsky posing in costume as the Faun. There was a flurry of excitement, but the film segments eventually proved to be computer-generated illusions, created by morphing existing photographs so that they appeared to be moving.

After the upheaval of World War I, when the Nijinsky era was over, the Ballets Russes found a home base in Monte Carlo and continued to experiment on the very cutting edge of modernism as Diaghilev engaged important avant-garde artists and composers for his productions. Among many others, Pablo Picasso and Henri Matisse, two of the greatest artists of the first half of the twentieth century, designed ballets for him.

After Diaghilev's death in 1929 of complications from diabetes—brought on by years of indulging in champagne, caviar, chocolate, and occasionally cocaine—the dancers and choreographers of the Ballets Russes scattered throughout the Western world. Tamara Karsavina settled in England to become one of the founders of modern British ballet. In the 1920s Bronislava Nijinska had become a major choreographer in her own right; her works include the masterpiece *The Wedding*, with music by Igor Stravinsky. She came to America in the late 1930s and settled in Los Angeles, where she choreographed for the movies and opened a ballet school. For decades Stravinsky enjoyed his position as one of the world's leading composers, constantly changing his style as he worked at the outer limits of his art. He eventually immigrated to America, where he was honored as a giant of classical music.

Both Kyra and Tamara Nijinsky eventually ended up in America as well. As she aged, an imperious Romola Nijinsky remained conscious of her husband's legacy. In the late 1960s, the Nijinsky name was once again in the news: Romola was thrilled when a Thoroughbred racehorse called Nijinsky became a great champion, winning the British triple crown. In her last years, Romola became a bit senile, and she finally died in Paris in 1978 at the age of eighty-seven.

Diaghilev's last choreographer was a young Russian named Giorgi Balanchivadze, who later made his way to America and cofounded the New York City Ballet under the name George Balanchine. He became perhaps the most important choreographer in the world during the last half of the twentieth century. The influence of the Ballets Russes ran deep and wide and still resonates today, one hundred years later.

In recent decades, as sexuality in general has become a civil-rights issue, and homosexuality has become widely acceptable, Nijinsky and Diaghilev have become gay icons, a concept that simply did not exist in the early twentieth century. They were the most celebrated gay couple of the Edwardian era. But Diaghilev was the real pioneer, making a point of living his life openly—the more passive Nijinsky simply followed in his wake.

Vaslav Nijinsky certainly was the greatest male dancer of his era. Some of the other Russian dancers may have been able to approach his impeccable technique, but eyewitnesses confirm over and over in the most emphatic terms possible that his dancing had a compelling and indefinable magic that transcended mere technique. He was equally gifted as an actor, inhabiting a role completely, becoming the character rather than just playing a part. Nijinsky radiated an unprecedented sexual magnetism onstage and may be regarded as one of the first real male sex symbols, with his innate physical ability to penetrate the subconscious of the audience and stir their most basic emotions using only his body.

Since Nijinsky, there have been many great dancers, but very few have had his kind of high-wattage star power, exceptions being Rudolf Nureyev (who, interestingly enough, was hailed as the new Nijinsky) and more recently, Mikhail Baryshnikov, who acted in films as well as danced. Both of these gifted artists were trained in the same grand Russian tradition that produced Nijinsky, and both defected from the Soviet Communist regime for greater artistic opportunities in the West.

As a creative artist, Nijinsky the choreographer made dances that were totally original, breaking every rule. He was decades ahead of his time, laying a foundation for modern dance—perhaps the most important part of his legacy. But Nijinsky's fame transcended even his art. Before social media, before the internet, before television, before radio, and before movies, there was only the stage. It was in the theater that Nijinsky became one of the first great celebrity performers of the twentieth century—a uniquely modern kind of superstar in the years right before technology provided mass entertainment to audiences of millions. Nijinsky's name, his brilliance as an artist, and his scandalous reputation were known by everyone, even though only live audiences—a relatively small number of people—ever saw him perform. In the end it was the catastrophe of his madness that assured his almost mythic status. He disappeared from public view and therefore never grew old in the popular imagination. His fabulous image, his scandalous notoriety, and his reputation as the world's greatest dancer were preserved, as one biographer noted, like "a fly caught in amber."

Rudolf Nureyev observed with some authority that Nijinsky's "mind broke because he could no longer dance." His sister, Bronia, who knew him best, wrote, "Without the theater Nijinsky withdrew into himself and closed the door to the realities of life, to abide in his own inner world of the dance." But perhaps Nijinsky's own words best capture his relationship to his art: "I gave my whole heart to it. I worked like an ox. I lived like a martyr."

Nijinsky in rehearsal clothes during the New York season, 1916

Painting of Vaslav Nijinsky as Petrushka

Author's Note

Nijinsky's life story is one of the best true stories in the world. Its plot is so sensational as to seem incredible.

—Lord David Cecil, historian

Nijinsky's life commands our attention by the sheer romantic force of its events. What a story this is! An awkward young boy who practically overnight becomes a world famous dancer, then creates three ballets that change dance history, then jilts the world's foremost ballet impresario, switches sexual orientations, marries a groupie, and goes raving mad, not without leaving behind an account of his conversations with God and a thorough inventory of his sexual practices.

—Joan Acocella, critic

Long before I knew his sensational life story, I was fascinated by photographs of Nijinsky. In the early 1970s, I was a young man living in New York City with an advanced art-history degree, trying to establish myself as a professional artist. I was attracted to a popular art movement of the day called photorealism. The idea was to reproduce the optical effect of a photograph in paint, to make an exact handmade copy, usually at a larger scale—an image of an image. I began to experiment, turning out quasi-photorealist paintings, refining my technique, and searching for my own style. I worked primarily from late nineteenth- and early twentieth-century black-and-white photos because I was drawn to their evocative lighting and fine detail. I soon abandoned trying to reproduce the effect of the old photos—I was much more interested in the human subjects and the graphic quality of their static poses. Departing from photorealism, I decided to elaborate upon the vintage photos. Making the figures life-size and in color gave the paintings a startling and vivid presence. During my exploration I came across a photo of Nijinsky as the Specter of the Rose. I was struck by the beautiful light as well as his androgynous pose. I had to paint him. This first Nijinsky painting was included in my debut exhibition as a professional artist in 1973.

After my one-man show, a friend gave me a book about the Ballets Russes. The photograph of Nijinsky as the Specter of the Rose was there, along with other photos of him in costume, as well as images of Fokine, Karsavina, Diaghilev, and Stravinsky. The Ballets Russes became my new subject. During the next year I created ten more life-size paintings, and there was a second one-man show in October 1974. These paintings caught the attention of the *New York Times*, and I was invited to show my work during the 1974–1975 winter season of the Joffrey Ballet at the New York City Center.

In the early 1990s, after twenty years as a professional gallery artist, I had the opportunity to illustrate a children's book. It turned out to be the beginning of a second career. For my second book I tried my hand at writing as well. I spent the next fifteen years writing and illustrating many nonfiction picture books for older kids. But Nijinsky lingered in my mind, and in 2008 I decided to make some new paintings of him. First I made a half-figure portrait of Nijinsky as Petrushka (p. 96), then a full-length canvas of Nijinsky as Harlequin (p. 41). Eventually there were six new life-size paintings. In the meantime, I had been reading everything I could get my hands on about Nijinsky and the Ballets Russes, and I became determined to write a biography for young adults. *The Great Nijinsky: God of Dance* is the result. After more than forty years, my two careers have merged, and my work has come full circle.

Nijinsky backstage with Diaghilev, Karsavina, and others after attending a performance of Petrushka, *1929*

The author with his painting The Afternoon of a Faun *(p. 55),*
New York City, 1974

Acknowledgments

I owe thanks to my lifelong friend Douglas Peix, who was there in the beginning and who encouraged me to become a painter; my friend George Shechtman, owner of Gallery Henoch, who long ago gave me my first chance as a professional artist and who exhibited my work for many years; Laura Geringer, who hired me for my first gig as a children's book illustrator; David Saylor, art director of my first four books, who steered an editor or two in my direction early on; Caitlyn Dlouhy, my wonderful editor at Atheneum, who kept the book contracts coming; the late George Nicholson, my literary agent, who believed in this project; and finally, Yolanda Scott, associate publisher and editorial director at Charlesbridge, who has worked closely with me to make this dream project a reality and whose creative input has been invaluable.

Nijinsky's Performances

During his career with the Ballets Russes, Nijinsky appeared in many ballets. Those featured in this book are only the best known. Below is a complete list of the ballets produced by Sergei Diaghilev in which Nijinsky danced. Some lasted only one season, while others became part of the repertoire of the Ballets Russes.

The Pavilion of Armida, 1909

A Banquet, 1909

Les Sylphides, 1909

Cleopatra, 1909

Carnaval, 1910*

Scheherazade, 1910

Giselle, 1910

Les Orientales, 1910

The Specter of the Rose, 1911

Narcissus, 1911

Petrushka, 1911

Swan Lake, 1911

The Blue God, 1912

The Afternoon of a Faun, 1912

Daphnis and Chloé, 1912

Jeux, 1913

The Rite of Spring, 1913

Till Eulenspiegel, 1916

*Nijinsky took on the role of Harlequin in 1911.

Ballet Performances Online

Although there are no movies of early Ballets Russes productions, nor any film of Nijinsky dancing, most of the ballets mentioned in this book may be seen in more recent productions on YouTube.

Of particular interest are recreations of the original productions of *Petrushka*, *The Afternoon of a Faun*, and *The Specter of the Rose*, featuring performances by Rudolf Nureyev in some of Nijinsky's most iconic roles, as well as the original choreography and scenic and costume designs. *The Rite of Spring* has also been recreated by the Joffrey Ballet with the original scenic and costume designs, but the choreography has been reimagined, since Nijinsky's choreography is lost. All the ballet music is available in many fine orchestral video performances and audio recordings on YouTube.

Finally, a search for Nijinsky finds film clips made from morphed still photos, which provide an eerie illusion, though perhaps not a realistic one, of Nijinsky dancing. Explore, and enjoy!

Source Notes

p. 1: "My senses . . . up there": Buckle, *Nijinsky*, pp. 102, 104.

p. 4: "regarded as . . . serious artistic expression": Scheijen, p. 114.

pp. 4–5: "When those . . . were on fire": Buckle, *Nijinsky*, p. 103.

p. 5: "Nijinsky took . . . supper and fame": Buckle, *Nijinsky*, p. 104.

p. 5: "wonder of wonders" and "God of the dance": Buckle, *Nijinsky*, p. 104.

p. 6: "No one . . . Ballets Russes": Kochno, p. 31.

p. 10: "feet pressed . . . against the other": Parker, p. 29.

p. 11: "The coming . . . more timely": Ostwald, p. 10.

p. 12: "In ten . . . our teeth": Buckle, *Nijinsky*, p. 9.

p. 12: "he seemed . . . a slow thinker": Ostwald, p. 11.

p. 12: "Japonczek" and "the little Japese": Buckle, *Nijinsky*, p. 8.

p. 12: "Are you . . . dance so well?": Ostwald, p. 11.

p. 12: "I know . . . my own eyes": Ostwald, p. 12.

p. 13: "I was ring-leader in many pranks": Ostwald, p. 13.

p. 16: "the energy . . . of beauty": Purvis et al., p. 8.

p. 16: "First of . . . of the arts": Scheijen, p. 74.

p. 17: "I finished . . . know life": Ostwald, p. 18.

p. 17: "I had my . . . cured of love": Moore, p. 33.

p. 19: "He loved . . . I loved him": Ostwald, p. 20.

p. 19: "I hated him . . . of luck": Moore, p. 49.

pp. 19–20: "I found luck . . . sacrifice I made": Moore, p. 49.

p. 26: "A harem . . . of vengeance": Scheijen, p. 201.

p. 27: "Now he was . . . pawing the ground": Buckle, *Nijinsky*, p. 160.

p. 27: "He was undulating . . . a reptile": Buckle, *Nijinsky*, p. 160.

p. 27: "I never . . . so beautiful": Buckle, *Nijinsky*, p. 161.

p. 27: "that he . . . an Indian Prince": Moore, p. 115.

p. 28: "A very rich . . . fresh poetry": Karthas, p. 83.

p. 30: "The transport of . . . his joy": Buckle, *Nijinsky*, p. 160.

p. 33: "Dressed modestly . . . his celebrity": Parker, p. 71.

p. 34: "Astonish me!": Scheijen, p. 323.

p. 36: "One would . . . the public": Ostwald, p. 48.

p. 36: "No, no . . . like it": Parker, pp. 132–133.

p. 36: "Nijinsky, even . . . as possible": Buckle, *Nijinsky*, p. 367.

p. 37: "a rather stocky . . . the background": Parker, p. 109.

p. 37: "dull and unintelligent": Parker, p. 109.

p. 37: "performed everything . . . his execution": Buckle, *Nijinsky*, p. 90.

p. 37: "order ruled . . . military precision": Buckle, *Nijinsky*, p. 90.

p. 37: "At these moments . . . new existence": Buckle, *Nijinsky*, p. 90.

p. 38: "an indecent and improper": Parker, p. 91.

pp. 38–39: "squirt water . . . bowing, smiling": Kopelson, p. 113.

p. 40: "An acrobatic . . . roar of applause": Parker, p. 104.

p. 42: "So loud . . . the music": Kochno, p. 65.

p. 46: "the finest actor in the world": Moore, p. 94.

p. 46: "Nijinsky succeeded . . . and Diaghilev?": Beaumont, pp. 361–362.

p. 46: "I used to . . . anyone in": Ostwald, p. 65.

p. 47: "As I was . . . every day": Ostwald, p. 65.

p. 47: "the mythical . . . of God": Moore, p. 95.

p. 48: "The great difficulty . . . *a puppet*": Buckle, *Nijinsky*, p. 230.

p. 54: "Nijinsky has . . . latest role": Buckle, *Nijinsky*, p. 286.

p. 58: "a fleeting . . . god of spring": Stravinsky, p. 31.

p. 59: "*Ras, dva, tri!*": Buckle, *Nijinsky*, p. 359.

p. 60: "Exactly what I wanted": Parker, p. 144.

p. 60: "the work of a madman": Hill, p. 116.

p. 61: "a twentieth-century . . . and visionary": Garafola, p. 74.

p. 61: "I began . . . with a stick": Ostwald, p. 73.

p. 61: "with the great . . . after him": Moore, p. 171.

p. 62: "Before I . . . mathematical gentleman": Buckle, *Nijinsky*, p. 341.

p. 64: "This is . . . a microscope": Buckle, *Nijinsky*, p. 356.

p. 68: "*Mademoiselle . . . moi?*" and "*Oui, oui, oui!*": Parker, p. 151.

p. 69: "overcome by . . . and shouting": Moore, p. xv.

p. 69: "I watched . . . into a madman": Acocella, "After the Ball Was Over."

p. 69: "gave himself . . . of dissipation": Ostwald, p. 92.

p. 70: "was to wear . . . with duchesses": Acocella, "After the Ball Was Over."

p. 70: "sandwiched between . . . and acrobats": Ostwald, p. 104.

pp. 74–75: "He is . . . at once" and "an impression . . . creative urge": Buckle, *Nijinsky*, p. 438.

p. 75: "Negro who . . . the princess": Moore, p. 188.

p. 75: "The moment . . . strange fancy": Moore, p. 188.

p. 78: "Mr. Nijinsky . . . medieval fantasy": *New York Times*, p. 14.

p. 82: "Now I will . . . its death": Moore, p. 203.

p. 83: "And we saw . . . the dead": Moore, p. 203.

p. 85: The chapter title "A Leap into Madness" is inspired by Ostwald's book title: *Vaslav Nijinsky: A Leap into Madness*.

p. 86: "I want . . . God Nijinsky": Nijinsky, pp. 145–146.

p. 86: "Wife, you . . . death warrant": Moore, p. 213.

p. 87: "Do not touch me!": Ostwald, p. 279.

p. 87: "would go . . . sugar solution": Acocella, "After the Ball Was Over."

pp. 87–88: "When we . . . a word": Ostwald, p. 262.

p. 91: "Ten years . . . in eclipse": Buckle, *Nijinsky*, p. 538.

p. 94: "a fly caught in amber": Moore, p. 261.

p. 95: "mind broke . . . no longer dance": Moore, p. 251.

p. 95: "Without the theater . . . the dance": Nijinska, p. 515.

p. 95: "I gave . . . a martyr": Moore, p. 119.

p. 97: "Nijinsky's life . . . seem incredible": Buckle, *Nijinsky*, back-cover promotional quotation.

p. 97: "Nijinsky's life . . . sexual practices": Acocella, "After the Ball Was Over."

Bibliography

Acocella, Joan. "After the Ball Was Over." *New Yorker*, May 18, 1992.

———. "The Faun." *New Yorker*, June 29, 2009.

———. "The Lost Nijinsky." *New Yorker*, May 7, 2001.

———. "Secrets of Nijinsky." *New York Review of Books*, January 14, 1999.

———. "The Showman." *New Yorker*, September 20, 2010.

Beaumont, Cyril. "Petrouchka." In *Reading Dance: A Gathering of Memoirs, Reportage, Criticism, Profiles, Interviews, and Some Uncategorized Extras*, edited by Robert Gottlieb, 360–365. New York: Pantheon, 2008.

Buckle, Richard. *Diaghilev*. London: Wiedenfeld and Nicholson, 1979.

———. *Nijinsky: A Life of Genius and Madness*. 3rd ed. New York: Pegasus Books, 2012.

Garafola, Lynn. *Diaghilev's Ballets Russes*. New York: Oxford University Press, 1989.

Hill, Peter. *Stravinsky: The Rite of Spring*. Cambridge, UK: Cambridge University Press, 2000.

Karthas, Ilyana. *When Ballet Became French: Modern Ballet and the Cultural Politics of France, 1909–1939*. Montreal: McGill-Queen's University Press, 2015

Kirstein, Lincoln. *Nijinsky Dancing*. London: Alfred A. Knopf, 1975.

Kochno, Boris. *Diaghilev and the Ballets Russes*. New York: Harper & Row, 1970.

Kopelson, Kevin. *The Queer Afterlife of Vaslav Nijinsky*. Stanford: Stanford University Press, 1997

Krasovskaya, Vera. *Nijinsky*. Translated by John E. Bowlt. New York: Schirmer Books, 1979.

Moore, Lucy. *Nijinsky*. London: Profile Books, 2013.

New York Times. "Portray in Ballet Strauss's Gay Tale." October 24, 1916.

Nijinska, Bronislava. *Early Memoirs*. Durham, NC: Duke University Press, 1981.

Nijinsky, Vaslav. *The Diary of Vaslav Nijinsky: Unexpurgated Edition*. Edited by Joan Acocella. New York: Farrar, Straus and Giroux, 1999.

Ostwald, Peter. *Vaslav Nijinsky: A Leap Into Madness*. New York: Carol Publishing Group, 1991.

Parker, Derek. *Nijinsky: God of the Dance*. Wellingborough, UK: Equation, 1988.

Purvis, Alston, Peter Rand, and Anna Winestein, eds. *The Ballets Russes and the Art of Design*. New York: Monacelli Press, 2009.

Scheijen, Sjeng. *Diaghilev: A Life*. New York: Oxford University Press, 2009.

Stravinsky, Igor. *An Autobiography*. New York: W. W. Norton, 1962.

Image Credits

Index

Page numbers in *italics* refer to illustrations.